THE CRAFTSMANSHIP REVIVAL
IN INTERIOR DESIGN

How Today's Artisans Preserve Yesterday's Skills

J. RONALD REED
WITH STEPHANIE CULP

HENRY HOLT AND COMPANY
NEW YORK

A FRIEDMAN GROUP BOOK

Copyright © 1989 by Michael Friedman Publishing Group, Inc.

Published by Henry Holt and Company, Inc.,
115 West 18th Street
New York, New York 10011

Library of Congress Cataloging-in-Publication Data
Reed, J. Ronald
The craftsmanship revival in interior design.
Includes index.
1. Decorative arts—Conservation and restoration—United States.
2. Interior architecture—Conservation and restoration—United
States. I. Culp, Stephanie.
II. Title.
NK805.R43   1988   729   88-6560
ISBN 0-8050-0518-8

Published simultaneously in Great Britain under the title
Authentic Craftsmanship in Interior Design.

First American Edition

THE CRAFTSMANSHIP REVIVAL IN INTERIOR DESIGN
How Today's Artisans Preserve Yesterday's Skills
was prepared and produced by
Michael Friedman Publishing Group, Inc.
15 West 26th Street
New York, New York 10010

Art Director: Mary Moriarty
Designer: Rod Gonzalez
Photo Editor: Christopher Bain
Production Manager: Karen L. Greenberg

Printed in Hong Kong

1 3 5 7 9 10 8 6 4 2

ISBN 0-8050-0518-8

Dedication

For those who value the discipline of craftsmanship that is
in itself an expression of human dignity. And to the
reasonable expectation that human dignity will continue to
demand that we create the best world possible.

Acknowledgments

Our greatest source of continuing knowledge is the library. Indeed, I have spent many pleasant hours in these institutions, researching and gathering information about the social development of civilization through the artistic expression of its craftspeople. It is important to acknowledge and gratefully thank the many librarians who helped me by patiently summoning forth books, which, for lack of popularity, had been cast into the basement or storage vaults. I am ever mindful of the fact that it is the librarian who has continued to quietly preserve the experiences and knowledge of our forefathers, long after wars and development schemes have erased their achievements from existence.

Secondly, I would like to thank Stephanie Culp, whose business skills and writing talents have made this book possible. Editor Karla Olson also deserves recognition for her patience, and for her own special "craftsmanship" skills, which are indelibly engraved upon the contents of this book. The photo research and organization by Chris Bain also stands as a significant contribution. And for grace under pressure typists Bonnie Sgarro and Judy Nelson get a thankful nod. Special thanks go to Mr. and Mrs. Arnold Culp, who offered the use of their cabin near Prescott, Arizona. It was in this beautiful setting, absent telephone and outside distractions, that many of our thoughts were turned into pages.

Special thanks must go to the craftspeople who so freely shared their time and expertise to benefit this project, and who are featured in this book. Their generosity and good manners were more than appreciated. Beyond that, it is the diligence, expertise, and curiosity of craftspeople such as these that, fortunately, keeps the values of craftsmanship alive and makes books such as this possible.

I would also like to acknowledge those who have made meaningful contributions to this book by sharing information, inspiration, or words of encouragement: Jeff Blydenburg, Mrs. R.B. Caldwall, Jean Grammer, Tom Michali, George Parker, Jr., Juan Sequeira, Allyne Winderman, and Cheryl Wilson. Thanks also go to the Booksville Bookstore, in Montrose, California, for taking the time to locate many obscure and out-of-print books for me.

Finally, acknowledgment is due to the countless number of guilds and associations who work to preserve the integrity of the past. Those deserving special mention here are the Canadian Victorian Society; the Guild of Master Craftsmen in Sussex, England; the National Parks Service; the New York Landmarks Commission; and the Artistic License (Guild) of San Francisco.

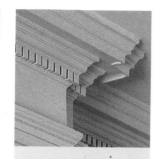

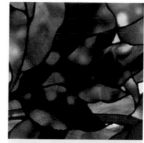

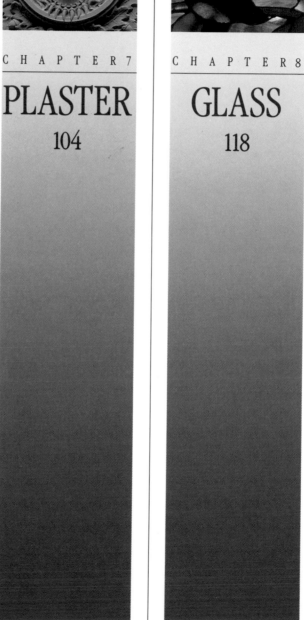

INTRODUCTION

Regardless of the historical period or culture, the design and process of making structures has almost always involved fulfilling human needs and ideas with the natural materials available. This, along with the human desire for beauty and self-expression, has been the cornerstone of craftsmanship in interior design throughout history.

The human ability to alter natural materials—stone, wood, and minerals—and shape them into objects of beauty, function, and protection provides the underlying motive of craftsmanship. The talent of the craftsperson to fashion trees into lumber, silicate into glass, clay into brick, minerals into paints, and rock into plaster has resulted in the elevation of these natural materials to art forms.

During Japan's Edo period and China's Ming Dynasty, the courtiers and warlords built beautifully crafted homes outside the perimeters of the Imperial Palace grounds. Similarly, the politicians and generals of the Roman Empire created spectacular seaside villas of the best craftsmanship. During the first century A.D., Pliny, a statesman of the Roman Empire, wrote:

"You may wonder why my Laurentine palace is such a joy to me. . . . but when you realize the attractions of the villa itself, the amenities . . . you will have your answer."

This busy administrator's home provided his family with a refuge of tranquility and harmony that only the elegance of the finest craftsmanship and decoration of the period could afford. This desire for tranquility and harmony in design has been present in many cultures. Throughout history, homes have been built of finely polished woods, as well as other beautifully worked natural resources. The elements in these homes have special meaning to their owners and reflect their ancestral and cultural history, as well as their social and religious philosophies.

The craftsmen of earlier periods often worked with precious and costly materials that had been brought from faraway lands at great expense. The elegance of nature was fine-tuned by the technical abilities of the well-trained craftsmen, with the same attention to detail given to everything, from the joinery of elegant paneling to the lowliest fitting. These finely crafted homes were built to stand for many generations, home to a family's families and beyond. There was no question that the utmost care and attention to detail be taken.

Today, the feeling of generational continuity in the form of long-standing households has all but disappeared. However, man's desire to associate with the expression of the artistic symbols of social standing and artistic achievement that fine craftsmanship represents is enjoying a revival today.

Just as the Renaissance man of bygone eras expressed his personal sense of accomplishment in the construction and decoration of his home, the Renaissance person of today also seeks the pleasure that comes from seeing and touching natural materials that have been manipulated by a master craftsperson into useful and beautiful objects.

This return to craftsmanship is not really new. History indicates that renewed interest in craftsmanship is cyclical, and as such, has been experienced at different times by various cultures. During periods of major social upheaval and strife, such as those marked by the wars of the Dark Ages and the World Wars, feelings of desperation are reflected in the minimalism of the interior design and decoration of architecture. It is during these times that craftsmanship and the sense of quality and beauty that accompany it are set aside as man works to heal the wounds of hate, sorrow, and suspicion. As societies gradually recover from war, however, the interest in craftsmanship begins to surface as cultures reestablish themselves with renewed vigor.

Another time when interest in authentic craftsmanship is renewed is when sameness replaces inventiveness, and the accepted styles of the day are so overworked that they become meaningless. For example, the Machine Age and industrialization brought mass production and served to diminish both the quality and integrity of the craftsmen that had preceded the machine. As industrialization became a more integral part of life, people gradually became more and more aware of the sacrifices it required and became dissatisfied with the instrument of newfound wealth—the machine. This discontent gave birth to the Arts and Crafts Movement, which was started by William Morris in England in the late 1800s. As a reaction to the mass-produced sameness that proliferated in interior design, this movement ushered in a return to the handcrafted furniture and architectural decorations that had once been commonplace. Unfortunately, the Arts and Crafts Movement did not last long, since the artistic, hand-applied process proved to be too expensive for most people. Consequently, craftsmanship within the decorative arts was to remain a toy of the wealthy until

Victoria & Albert Museum

it was revived for a short time during the Art Deco period.

The current revival of craftsmanship can likewise be viewed as a result of a rebellious attitude against the technology that is so prevalent today. Weary of modern design, many people are exploring the possibility of incorporating authentic craftsmanship into the contemporary design of their homes. Owners of older homes steeped in history are seeking to uphold the traditions by restoring the authentic interior decorative arts that surround them.

Unfortunately, however, the economics of today's industrial world has made it almost impossible to maintain an independent, one-of-a-kind craft workshop. Mass-produced goods are almost always instantly available at a cost generally much less than the overall cost of the work delivered by the craftsperson. The talent required to execute authentic decorative arts requires an extensive background not only in a particular craft, but in history of design and scientific technology as well. This, along with the considerable talents of the craftsperson, the expense of authentic or quality materials, and the time required to perform the craft artistically and accurately all but guarantee that authentic craftsmanship for any given project will not be acquired at bargain rates.

Despite this, budgetary concerns can, to some extent, be applied to any given project without completely eliminating the services of the craftsperson. Setting priorities for the stages of the project is an important first step. If the project has several areas where work needs to be done, completing the whole project in a series of stages can be helpful, as well. Tackling one room at a time, for example, or doing one specific area first, such as the ceilings, might be the answer to working within financial constraints. Mixing the old with the new, such as craftsmanship with cost-saving newer materials, often provides an overall price reduction in the project.

Whatever your financial concerns, clearly explain them to the craftsperson you are working with at the start of the project. Often the craftsperson will have ideas and know options that can be helpful in terms of the total project cost. Unfortunately, you may discover that your project would suffer irreversibly from any budgetary constraints, and because of this, the only solution may well be to wait until funds are available to do the job properly, without scrimping. In any event, by first thoroughly discussing budget concerns and everything involved—from the materials used to the time required of the craftsperson—you will be spared any unhappy financial surprises as the project progresses.

Budgetary concerns for the project are but one of the aspects that go into the decision to use the services of a craftsperson. Your relationship with the craftsperson can also be critical to the success of the project. The craftsperson's artistic interpretation may be very different from your original vision of the project, unless the expected outcome of the project is explored in detail and in advance by everyone concerned. Clipping pictures from magazines or providing photographs or drawings can help you to clearly explain your expectations. Also, your selection of a craftsperson should take into account his or her work and whether or not it is compatible with your original design concept. It is important to determine whether the craftsperson's style of work will blend with any historical requirements of the project in question. In the end, however, while an agreement regarding the

*T*his
Romanesque dome ceiling incorporates several of the decorative crafts, including gilded bas-relief plaster work and hand-painting (left). Elegant repeated patterns of leading in the window provide a complementary frame for the stained glass roundel at the bottom (above).

*T*his
beautifully crafted tri-column provides support to the City Hall in Rochester, New York (page 6). Craftspeople reviving authentic techniques have found that an important forum for their work is public buildings that are protected as historic landmarks.

*W*illiam
Morris's lush designs of the Arts and Crafts Movement reached back to the richness of artisanry before the Industrial Revolution and the age of mass production (page 7).

A

*raised frieze applied to the upper edge
of a wall makes the ceiling appear
higher. This crown design in a durable
paper product called Lincrusta imitates
the intricacy of a carved plaster
decoration without the expense.*

Intricately

*handcarved and augmented wood
doors, doorframes, and moldings that
combine classic French curves and
Chinese accents provide a rich
backdrop for the treasures displayed in
this hallway (right). The repeated
corner pieces make the hall appear
longer than it is.*

Craftsman

*Alan Bird uses a chisel and mallet to
carve a stone capital (far right).*

Courtesy Stoneyard Institute/© Robert F. Rodriguez

overall scope of the design should be reached, it is the personal expression of the artist that will make the project unique, and it is a mistake to totally suppress this talent in an effort to get exactly what you think you want.

To find the right craftsperson for a given project, check with a preservation group or craft guild in your area. Often these groups can provide you with the names of craftspeople who specialize in the work that is required for your project. It is important to understand that artists' guilds are not the same as craft guilds.

Many people believe that artists or art students can perform the crafts required for interior decorative arts. This is a mistake. Artists not trained in the historical and technical aspects of the decorative arts are simply not qualified to tackle architectural projects. By the same token, doing any of the work yourself can also be fraught with hazards. If, however, you are determined to do part of the work yourself, you will want to be certain that anything you attempt is reversible. With that in mind, it is also important to know that performing a Band-Aid job on a restoration project—whether you attempt to do it yourself, or you have a local workman attempt it— more often than not creates a much more expensive problem later.

The craftsperson whom you finally select should have a proven background that includes artistic, historical, and technical expertise. Requesting photographic evidence of the craftsperson's past projects is reasonable. Many vendors of authentic or replication materials have catalogs; sometimes they require a small fee in return.

Once you have selected a craftsperson, you will want to plan the work

schedule. Be prepared to contract the craftsperson's services well in advance, since he or she may already be working on another project and, therefore, will not be available for your project for several months. Find out what the special needs of the craftsperson are, and if you have other work going on in the house, work with the craftsperson on a specific schedule for his or her portion of the work. For example, a craftsperson usually cannot work if plaster dust is in the air (the dust contaminates the work he or she is doing), and if rooms are being spray painted, virtually no one but the painters can work because of the fumes. Additionally, in many of the authentic crafts, time is required for drying, and during that drying time, it is important that no dust or debris from other work be floating in the air, since it will ruin the surfaces that are drying.

If your project is an expensive one, acknowledge your agreement with the craftsperson for the project by signing a drawing or blueprint of the work to be done. This will help ensure that the project will conform to your original vision within an agreed-upon price.

Ultimately, your decision to use a craftsperson is a personal one. The results of his or her work will provide the permanent background for your everyday life, and your relationship with that environment is a key factor that should be considered in your relationship with the craftsperson. Finally, the value of your home should increase proportionately with the value of the work done, and you will be able to experience the lifelong reward that comes with the daily exposure to the long overdue and warmly welcomed craftsmanship revival in interior design.

METAL

Metals have many characteristics that have made them valuable to man throughout the growth of civilization. They are very hard, yet when heated they can be molded, cast, or hand-beaten into any shape, and sharpened, which ancient man recognized as an important asset for developing tools, weapons, and decorations. The beauty and economic value of metals added to man's fascination with them.

Little is known about the earliest metal craftsmen from the Iron and Bronze Ages. The various isolated cultures of the East and West independently discovered the art and science of metallurgy. The Greeks and Romans learned their craft from the early Egyptians, whose techniques included the making of gold death masks. Metal craftsmen throughout the Roman Empire began shaping and casting metal objects of every description. The metal pieces were then decorated with cut, pierced, and engraved patterns. Another technique was to inlay the metal pieces with other

Courtesy Klahm & Sons Inc., Ornamental Metalsmiths

The classic trellis design *of these leaded glass windows is enhanced by the* trompe l'oeil *scene on the back wall (right). Nature almost literally enters into this garden room.*

The fine art of the metalwork in this domed window is as important and as beautiful as the stained glass it supports. (Far right, above: metalwork by Klahm & Sons.)

This Art Deco bird wrought out of iron is reminiscent of a design found in ancient Celtic and French Gothic decorative patterns (far right, below).

Guests are greeted with drama and beauty at this California home (page 13; metalwork by Klahm and Sons).

colored metals in delicate patterns. This work is known as damasking. Hammered metal, called repoussé, was made into every possible shape.

With the development of specialized techniques, metal became a symbol of affluence. The doorknocker was a prized household possession greatly favored by both the Greeks and Romans. The Jews established themselves as specialists in decorated metal for personal use. Gradually, decorative hinges, escutcheons, nails, and polished metal mirrors were used and displayed as symbols of success, power, and wealth.

The Greeks were probably first to standardize the use of metal to create a Western coinage and monetary system. Naturally, advanced metal crafts were used to service the military also. Spearheads, breastplates, helmets, armbands, batallion insignias, and chariot parts were hand wrought from metal.

Iron has long been the chief metal used in construction, with the people of Mesopotamia, Egypt, Greece, and Rome all using iron decoratively as well as to hold columns together, fasten wood construction materials, and keep roofing tiles attached.

Yet perhaps nothing exemplifies the importance of metal to man more than the nail. During the centuries, nails have been made in every conceivable shape and size: round, square, long, short, small, large, and extra large. Some cultures went to great lengths to make finishing nails with decorative heads for doors and furniture. These decorative nails were usually made by heating the smelted wire or rod and hand beating the head into the desired shape. Today, although there are a few companies that still make reproduction nails (particularly from the Colonial period), nails are made almost exclusively by modern machinery. The decorative nail head is now a separate detail that is usually added after the furniture, door, staircase (or whatever) is assembled, and then is used only for ornamentation.

Because of their beautiful colors, copper and copper alloys of brass and bronze have always been the favored metals for decorative purposes. Copper is a base metal.

When it is combined with zinc, the result is brass; when mixed with tin, it becomes bronze.

For centuries, copper and its alloys have been used in a wide variety of architectural styles to make decorative hardware. Copper is normally considered informal; golden brass adds a regal air; deep-toned bronze is almost always restricted to formal applications.

Brass was accidentally discovered by an alchemist who was attempting to create gold. It quickly became a favorite metal of the Greeks and Romans, who considered it very valuable. Originally it was used to make things that were to be prominently displayed, advertising wealth and social position. When the brass doorknocker was created, one of the earliest designs was, most appropriately, the suspended hand and forearm. Doorknockers were eventually made in a variety of designs scaled with the door and in keeping with the status of the household.

During the Dark Ages, the metal craftsmen were kept busy making beautifully decorated coats of armor and shields to be used in battle. Along with the stone walls, columns, arches, and slate roofs of Gothic architecture went metal fasteners, including nails, bands, shafts, and retainer pins.

The metal crafts of the Dark Ages were more practical than ornamental art forms. Even the artistic elongated hinge tails that were as wide as the door to which they were affixed were actually a part of the support system to keep the wooden door pieces together.

In Moorish Spain, wrought-iron workers fashioned ornamental iron parts for use as security bars in windows and as gates. The need for security and protection against thievery also demanded locks, keys, and decorative window bars and grills to replace the wooden slide locks that offered little, if any, resistance to intruders. The Moors followed the examples of artisans in the Ottoman Empire, who made security windows from delicately wrought iron grillework that looked as fine and fragile as lace but were strong enough to prohibit unwanted visitors from entering.

Meanwhile, the craftsmen involved in church construction made leaded framing for stained glass windows, and iron hinges and pulls for the massive doors and window shutters. In medieval castles, special hooks and metal racks appeared for storing cooking utensils, livery, and other items that could be hung on the walls or from the ceiling. As the middle class evolved and grew in number, strength, and wealth, so did the demand for decorative metal household objects. Hinges, door-locking bars, grilles, grates, window bars, hasps, and hooks were only a few of the items handcrafted from metal.

Courtesy Klahm & Sons Inc., Ornamental Metalsmiths

The Renaissance Italians revived brass and bronze as a favorite household accent. The Italians passed their preference for brass and bronze door and cabinetry hardware on to the French, who made brass and light-colored bronze extremely fashionable, creating countless brass and bronze architectural ornamentations and fittings. This taste for brass and bronze eventually made its way to England, where, during the Georgian period, these metals were put to extensive decorative use. Most of the Classical Revival dwellings were fitted with brass and bronze hardware that included doorknobs, hinges, locks, fingerplates, corner guards, rails, and other trims that were functional, protected the wood, or provided architectural definition.

With the opening of the ports of Japan to the West in the 1700s, the European craftsmen learned of new metal technology. The centuries-old Japanese Samurai tradition had highly stylized decorations, particularly on weapons and uniforms. Japan was in the golden Edo period of its arts, and Europeans were impressed not only with the

© Carole Graham/FPG International

elegant craftsmanship but also with the technology of Japanese sword making. The Samurai sword blade was the best in the world—the prototype of stainless steel blades. In household items, the refined ornamentations of the Japanese included hinges made in the likeness of butterfly wings or plum blossoms, and cabinet parts and corner guards in the shape of honeysuckle, wisteria, and hundreds of other objects of nature.

Metal has long been used for the fireplace. Andirons were designed to prevent burning logs from rolling onto the hearth and into the room. Metal mesh, or mail, had also been used as a part of armor, and it replaced hand-woven fireplace screens that were originally made from wicker. Many fireplaces in Europe and the colonial provinces were large enough to accommodate a stove and oven for baking as well as provide heat for the house. Many of these fireplaces were fitted with a caldron and a soup pot, both made of iron. Pokers were created to help maintain the fire and to aid with the cooking.

In the late 1700s the French developed the first automated metal-processing equipment. A water wheel was connected to a "hammer" wheel with a long wooden shaft—a system very similar to a grinding mill. The metalsmith controlled the continuously turning hammer wheel by applying pressure to a rope wrapped around it, lowering or raising the pounding device as needed. This method was quickly adopted by the English, and became known as "rope drop" work. A great deal of skill was required to control the rope drop stamp hammer properly, as it did not have variable speeds or other adjustments.

With the invention of the room-heating stove by Benjamin Franklin in the New World, iron started to be used in a major way for heat. The Franklin stove with pipes replaced the traditional fireplace. This heating system, in turn, was succeeded by the steam-heat system with iron radiators and registers to carry the heat throughout the dwelling.

In the American South, wrought iron was a favored accent for most well-to-do homes during the 1800s. Craftsmen of the period followed the Spanish styles that had originated with the Moors, and made cast iron winding staircases, banisters, columns and poles, capitals, brackets, gates, fences, and grillework.

After the Chicago fire of 1871, in which 17,500 structures burned in one night and over 100,000 people were left homeless, society looked for methods of construction to prevent such catastrophes. Brick became a preferred building material, and machine-pressed sheet metal was used for wainscots, ceilings, cornice moldings, and chair rails. Exterior uses for metal included roofing shingles,

Courtesy Klahm & Sons Inc., Ornamental Metalsmiths

finials, friezes, roof ribs, drains, and rain spouts. All of these decorations were made in every imaginable Gothic and Classic design. Many ceilings from the turn of the century still exist in historic, particularly commercial, structures, testimony to the durability of the material.

The Victorian metal craftsmen inherited a legacy of excellence from the Georgian period, during which the hardware in England, America, and Canada was most lavishly designed. Age-old patterns from many different nations were used and often combined with each other. The discipline of the Edo period of Japanese architectural ornamentation also had a great influence on Victorian styles, the Arts and Crafts Movement, and many twentieth-century American designs.

The *majestic strength of metal is combined with the softness and beauty of wood in this modern interpretation of a classic staircase banister (above, metalwork by Klahm and Sons).*

The *art and technology of wrought iron is displayed here by the elegant and beautiful supports for this ceiling (left). To save money and simplify upkeep, the look of leaded glass has been replicated on plastic sheets.*

*M*aster
metalsmiths, Jack (left) and Alex (right)
Klahm work together to shape a piece
of metal in their foundry (below).

*T*his
sign bracket (bottom) was reproduced
by Klahm and Sons from a
nineteenth-century original. The
craftwork combines forged support
bars, cast dragon motif,
hand-hammered repoussé leaves, and a
special 23K goldleaf overlay.

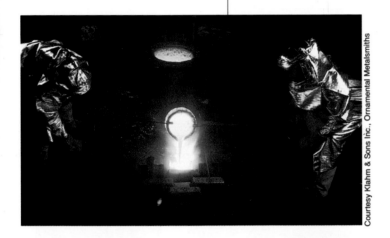

ALEX AND JACK KLAHM

For three generations, the Klahm family name has stood for quality custom metal work. Alex and Jack Klahm's grandfather started working with metal in Germany, where he was a blacksmith and machinist. Now in America, their father picked up the trade and for thirty years he taught blacksmithing, foundry, drafting, sheet metal layout, copper work, and repoussé. When he retired, Alex and Jack, who had grown up in their father's shop, assumed responsibility for Klahm and Sons, Inc.

Located in Ocala, Florida, Klahm and Sons maintains a foundry where they do their own forge and cast work in iron, bronze, brass, and copper. Here, Alex and Jack combine creative design with traditional craftsmanship to provide ornamentation for both interior and exterior architectural requirements.

The Klahms make it a point to work together with the client to create a design that will suit the client's personal, as well as architectural, needs. Drawings that convey the mood of the project represent a first step in the design that is then subject to sculptural interpretation in the foundry. How the metal will be perceived in its final form is also considered. While metal is often used to make barriers, the Klahm's artistic designs can result in a gate, for example, that is such a source of beauty that the beholder temporarily forgets that the purpose of the piece is to inhibit entry.

The Klahms are master metalsmiths, and restoration and reproduction represent a part of the work that they do. Still, preserving the past does not mean that they are tied to it. Convinced that they are limited only by their imaginations, the Klahms are apt to use metal that has been discarded, such as an old pot bellied stove, and turn it into a modern metal piece that will grace a stairway in a contemporary home. Whatever design or reproduction they create, they say that what they have achieved has come from "the skill of the human hand, an eye for detail, a love of artistic metalwork, and the most basic of tools: hammer, anvil, and fire."

Their achievements are many and include, in Hawaii, the restoration of the ironwork in the fence around the Ilonai Palace, the restoration of the 1867 iron gates and fencing guarding the Royal Mausoleum, and the design and creation of an entry for the 1837 Palace in Kailua-Kona. Other creations include three six foot hand-forged chandeliers that hang in a country club in Atlanta, Georgia, a grand staircase with a brass cap rail for a 14,000 square foot private residence in Sarasota, Florida, and an award winning door that is currently at the National Ornamental Metal Museum in Memphis, Tennessee.

The
band-wrought iron scroll work in this
chandelier and banister revives an
ancient craft complementary to a
contemporary interior. (Left:
metalwork by
Klahm and Sons.)

Unique
metal foliation adds design integrity
and impact to a banister. (Below:
metalwork by Klahm and Sons.)

Well-executed pierced metalwork combines with repoussé to form a handsome fireplace screen.

Classifications and Applications

Metal is found in abundant quantities in deposits of ore or rocks containing high levels of minerals. By crushing the rock and heating it to high temperatures, the oxygen is removed from the metal oxide crystal, which causes it to melt into a liquid that separates from the crushed rock. This process is called smelting. The furnace, called a smelter, is normally constructed so that the molten metal ore is collected at the bottom of the furnace.

Metal can be classified into two basic categories: ferrous and nonferrous. The word *ferrous* is derived from the Latin word *ferrum,* which means iron. All iron and iron alloys are considered to be ferrous metals, while copper, lead, zinc, tin, and aluminum are nonferrous metals. Another method of classifying metals is by differentiating pure metals from metal alloys. Pure metal is any base metal, or a metal made up of only one chemical element, such as iron, copper, lead, zinc, tin, and aluminum. Alloys are metals, such as bronze, brass, or steel, that contain more than one metal.

Regardless of its classification, metal was mostly made into bars, rods, or sheets in a foundry. Craftsmen nor-mally worked with a very hot bed of coals rigged with a large set of bellows making a forge. The metal was heated until it became hot enough to bend into the desired shape. Different types, sizes, and shapes of hammer heads were used, depending on the work to be performed.

Brass was made through a similar process and cast or hammered into relief patterns to form a decorative panel that was usually glued or nailed to a wood surface (such as a door). Although some pierced metal pieces were made during the colonial period, this was usually limited to the plates that surrounded locks (escutcheons), drawer pulls, hinge tails, and hasps. Pierced metal designs were made by hand-cutting, drilling, and sawing patterns into the formed, cooled, and cut metal. These pieces were usually finished by filing away any burrs or untidy edges, then polishing the item.

Bronze was shaped by casting. Appropriate for Classical design, it eventually became a preferred metal in commercial structures, especially alongside marble, and was often seen in public offices and other institutions.

Originally, designs in metal were hammered and bent by hand. Weathervanes, for example, were cut with snips and hand sawn. They were then smoothed with a file and shaped with a mallet and chasing tools on the metalsmith's anvil and chasing pad. Repoussé, or embossed, metal was also done completely by hand, with the metal normally worked from the back side first. The metal sheet was placed over a container filled with a substance that would allow each blow of the hammer to make an impression while providing resistance. For example, the French used black pitch mixed with tallow and plaster of paris. The pitch pot was always hemispherical in shape so that it could be placed into a chaser's ring and turned at any angle. The relief work was dented out from the back side to make the raised relief pattern, and then turned over and hammered and detailed according to the design wanted. The tools for repoussé include a selection of hammer heads, chasing tools, engravers, and punches. Many tools of the authentic style are still used today, a standard set including over fifty pieces in different sizes and shapes.

In the metal-casting process, molten metal is poured into a mold, then cooled to take the shape of the mold. Most metal molds are made from a mixture of sand and clay, a type used through the centuries. Another common mold, used for jewelry, is the investment, or lost wax, mold. To make this mold, a sculpted wax image is made and set into a container that is then filled with a silicate compound that is allowed to harden. This mold is heated to about 1,500°F (815°C) and turned upside down so that the melted wax runs out of the investment. The molten metal is poured into the mold while it is still hot, permitting the metal to flow into the finer details of the mold. The third type of mold commonly used for metal casting is one made of plaster. Usually a wooden model is carved, then plaster of paris is mixed and poured over the mold and allowed to set. The mold is allowed to dry thoroughly, usually for several weeks. Plaster molds have been popular for bronze ornamentation and statuary when only one casting was desired.

Although the methods for making molds have changed little over the centuries, the forge has basically become obsolete. Today, many artisans operate only a small gas-fueled furnace, sufficient for metals that have lower melting temperatures, such as copper, brass, bronze, aluminum, and zinc. For the metals that require higher heats to come to a pouring temperature, most artisans opt to make their own mold models, and turn the rest of the work over to a foundry.

Except for a few ornamental pieces, metal craftsmanship has given way to the machine, and the craftspeople have gradually become machinists, operating power stamping and cutting equipment to shape and decorate iron, tin, galvanized steel, and copper. Though craftspeople still do repoussé work, more often than not machinery now stamps and embosses the patterns onto most panels. Many patterns can be ordered as stock items today. Most stock patterns, however, lack the individuality and uniqueness of custom work.

Magnificent metal craftsmanship belies the practical aspects of this restored Victorian fireplace (c1876). The hand-cut surrounds of purple-veined marble reflect Gothic designs that were popular in the nineteenth century.

This bandcrafted metal banister extends the baroque style of the mirror and console in this entry. The top of the bandrail reflects light from the chandelier.

Restoration Guidelines

The art of decorative metal is, strictly speaking, not suitable for a do-it-yourself project. Because of the high temperatures required to soften metal, this craft is generally considered beyond the average homeowner's capabilities. Attempting to bend the metal by hand is never advisable. Although most metals can be bent without heating, this causes stress at the point of the bend, ultimately weakening the integrity of the piece.

Modern equipment, originally developed during the Machine Age, eliminates the need for deep beds of burning coal. Torches with gas cylinders and specially constructed ovens heat the metal to make parts for architectural ornamentation. Many of these parts and patterns have become standardized in response to heavy demand.

Decorative cast-iron pieces for almost any use can now be ordered from catalogs. Scrolls for bannisters, entire cast-iron staircases, counter and shelving supports and brackets, gates and window grilles, along with elaborate registers, are but some of the many cast-iron pieces that can be ordered in this manner. Brass fixtures, hinges, and hasps can be purchased, as well as tin ceiling and wainscot panels that are faithful reproductions of the originals.

Cast-iron and metal parts, such as for a staircase, are usually joined either mechanically with fasteners, screws, rivets, or wire, or by brazing and welding. The average homeowner does not have either the skills or the equipment to attach the metal where these sophisticated techniques are required. On the other hand, if all that is needed is screw fasteners, some clamps and vises can be combined with a little ingenuity to drill the necessary holes for the fasteners. Whether you or a professional installs the ornamentation, by including any number of these premade patterns into your overall design, costs can be controlled significantly.

Custom-designed and assembled wrought iron also involves the time and talents of a craftsperson. Wrought iron is formed from flat bars of iron. The craftsperson first heats the iron enough to allow the metal to be bent. The artisan usually predetermines the curve or angle that is desired, and, by clamping one end of the heated bar in a vise, can then work the metal into the necessary shape. The heated portion can also be placed against an anvil and hammered into shape. With this method, the craftsperson uses a pair of tongs to hold the heated metal while he or she pounds and bends it.

If you are not familiar with an independent craftsperson who can do the metal work you desire, many local

© Bill Rothschild/Kleiman & Valente, designers

foundries have experienced craftspeople to make the models for reproduction or custom-designed architectural ornamentations. Once you decide you want a handcrafted original or reproduction design, you still have some cost-effective options. You may want to collaborate with the craftsperson and select from catalogs some items such as machine-formed leaves, flowers, crests, lions, or other motifs that can be combined with the twists, scrolls, and other designs that the craftsperson can use to complete your project. Historic or preservation consultants, architects who are familiar with authentic design, and a metal craftsperson can all coordinate and work together on your project to provide a unique architectural decoration.

Sometimes, all that is needed to make authentic metalwork look almost new again (remember, metal is a very durable material), is a good cleaning. Metal can be cleaned with a mild soap and water solution, using a natural bristle brush. After you have cleaned the metal, dry it with a lint-free cloth to prevent water from puddling and causing rust. Once the metal is completely dry, saturate a lint-free cloth with an oil, such as lemon, almond, or linseed, then rub the metal to apply a thin, even, protective coating. Be careful not to saturate the cloth with oil; this will leave excess deposits of oil on the metal surface that will eventually become gummy and collect dust.

Metal arts have been a useful and artistic form for interior design for centuries, bringing beauty, comfort, and function into daily life. Replaced by machines, metalsmiths who wrought and engraved metal into artful forms have, in most cases, become a part of history. Today, those who choose to carry on this custom craft are guaranteed a place in history for passing on the craft that came from those before them.

TREMONT NAIL COMPANY

© Christopher Bain

Tremont Nail Company has a history that goes back well over 125 years. Located at the gateway to Cape Cod, near historic Plymouth, Massachusetts, some of the buildings at the Tremont plant were built as early as 1848. Tremont Nail Company is America's oldest manufacturer of cut nails, which they still produce in twenty different patterns on machinery that is over 100 years old.

Originally established by the Tobey family, the company was bought in 1927 by James S. Kenyon, who passed it along to his son. When James, Jr. died, his wife, Charlotte, took over. Helping her run Tremont is Donald Shaw, a childhood friend of her husband's and president and general manager of Tremont for the past twenty-two years.

Machinist and foreman, Ted Roy is one of thirty-two employees at Tremont. Roy joined Tremont in 1934 when he was seventeen years old. Today he can do just about any job in the plant, but his major responsibility is the upkeep of the equipment. When a machine breaks down, it's Roy's job to locate the problem and fix it. If a new part is needed for any of the authentic machines, he makes a new casting at the Tremont foundry.

On hand to help and learn from Ted Roy is blacksmith Gary Franklin. Twenty-five years old, Franklin is the fifth generation of his family to be a nailer at Tremont, and he often works alongside his father, who is sixty-one years old. To make a part for the machinery, Franklin and Roy make a pattern that is hand cast and heated in the forge. The part is then shaped, with one of them holding it on the anvil, while the other swings the sledge hammer.

It is those carefully maintained and operated machines that turn out the very special cut nails at Tremont. Cut nails possess great durability. They are hard to pull out and do not loosen easily because the wood fibers are pushed downward and wedge against the nails, which prevents loosening. Today, Tremont's cut nail patterns include (among others): the common nail *for framing, roughing, floors, and sculpturing;* the floor nail *for laying tongue and groove flooring;* the masonry nail *for nailing furring strips and other material to cinder block, mortar joints, and brick walls;* the decorative wrought head, *designed to simulate the hand-forged nail of the late 1700s;* the hinge nail *for fastening antique hinges;* and the fine finish nail *for furniture repair, cabinet work, paneling, and casings.*

As long as the machines keep running smoothly, the discriminating craftspeople who contact Tremont will be able to receive the authentic nails that they need to complete their handcrafted projects. And Ted Roy and Gary Franklin both plan to continue playing an active role in the continuing history of Tremont. When asked how much longer they'd be at the Tremont Nail Company, both Franklin and Roy indicated that they'd be making nails at Tremont for as long as Tremont would let them.

HARDENED STEEL

The
Tremont Nail Company has been
making nails from this location
for over 125 years.

PAINT

Since the times of the prehistoric cave drawings, man has been painting and decorating his dwellings with symbols of his mystical relationship with nature. As civilizations developed, man continued to use color and decorative arts to enhance household utensils, pottery, clothing, as well as dwellings. Gradually, early man's symbolism evolved into more complex decorations that were used to beautify tombs, religious sites, throne rooms, and other seats of power. With the eventual establishment of a middle class, the painted decorative arts blossomed into an expression of the artistic integrity of individual achievement.

By the time Alexander the Great had established himself as the King of Kings in the eastern Mediterranean, the craftsmen of the courts of that area had already been using decorative paints, gilding, silver foil, hand-painted tiles, stenciling, painted friezes, and borders to glorify and decorate their great halls of power. During Alexander's reign, the

Detail and precision of design and application lend unique beauty to handprinted wallpaper (right). These papers are expensive, so if cost is a concern, consider featuring a border as an accent on a painted wall.

Stencil art with hand-painted insets (previous page) makes use of a historic color palette along with gilded embellishments to create this neoclassic motif adapted for contemporary interior design (craftsmanship by: Larry Boyce & Associates).

capital cities of Western civilization came under the protection and convenience of standardized coinage. As a result, the craftsmen of these cities and countries were able to exchange ideas and materials more easily. They perfected and popularized their crafts, which became part of the Greek classical art period.

The craftsmen of this period got the basis of their knowledge and technique from the expertise of the ancient Egyptian tomb painters and stuccoists, as well as from the talents of the Persian and Assyrian decorative artists. Rejecting the formal conventionalism of the stiff, religious art and formal official style that were typical of that time, the Greek Empire artists developed a more natural style. At the same time, they adopted the color palettes of the Eastern countries. The resulting style of art was later adapted by the conquering Romans, and it was quickly spread throughout the Roman Empire.

With the collapse of the Roman Empire, the northern European countries slipped into 900 years of war and superstition—years that were basically devoid of scientific and artistic development. Nevertheless, during these Dark Ages, the craft of the stencil artist replaced that of the muralist and managed to reach remarkable levels of expression and ornamentation. The trend of the period was to build fortresses with plain walls covered with plaster. These walls were usually painted or stenciled with various types of repeat geometric patterns, foils, heraldic motifs, and arches or other references to architectural details.

Throughout the Dark Ages, the decorative artist survived by pleasing the lord or local abbot, who, in turn, provided him with secure housing, food, and an annuity. The church system remained a valuable source of training and knowledge. Frequently, an abbey in England that needed a specific artistic service to be done requested that an artist with the appropriate talents be sent from an abbey in France where this type of work had been done. This exchange system applied to crafts such as gilding, wood carving, and stone carving, as well as many others.

In Italy, the decorative art masters of Rome remained

in demand, primarily to paint decorations on the walls of churches and halls of the warlords who ruled the land on which they lived. The competitiveness among Italian families kept the fresco painters, stencilists, and mosaic artists busy decorating the palaces of Florence, Pisa, Venice, Sienna, and Bologna, where spacious rooms reflected the colorations and flamboyance of Byzantine architecture and taste.

During the Middle Ages, it was the merchant class that established a wealthy citizenry in Italy. The road to riches in the northern European countries lay with a court appointment, where the opportunities to extract bribes and other forms of graft lined the pockets of a lucky few. With this money, court appointees were able to acquire great estates, which they lavishly decorated using all of the architectural crafts at their disposal. The walls and ceilings of these estates were painted gloriously, and today these estates are often viewed as magnificent examples of human ingenuity and the integrity of craftsmanship. In their day, however, the majority of the population saw them differently—as symbols of aristocratic and bureaucratic corruption.

During this period, the northern Europeans were plagued by attacks from nomadic tribes. As their cities were burned and pillaged, they rebuilt them with stone fortresses in a style that became known as Gothic. Interior architectural decorations in these fortresses were generally found only in the great hall or throne room, and were usually limited to stenciling and painted ornamentation on the flat plaster walls and, occasionally, on the beams of the ceilings.

In England, the Gothic movement took on a unique and naturalistic style, featuring intertwined vines and floral motifs. The borders and patterns that the English craftsmen were painting were mostly based on these wickerlike patterns that originated with the arts and crafts of their Celtic ancestors.

These decorative practices continued to expand to include murals and Italian perspective painting. This became known as *trompe l'oeil,* which means to fool the eye, and is a special technique of painting flat surfaces to achieve three-dimensional visual effects. This painting technique, when used to replicate the patterns and colorations of marble and woods on a plaster surface, has come to be known as marbleizing and wood graining.

The Italian artist of the sixteenth century Michelangelo is probably the best known trompe l'oeil painter. In one of his most famous works, he ignored the shape of the Sistine Chapel ceiling and fooled the eye by painting imaginary architectural shapes and figures onto flat sur-

faces. The result is that the ceiling seems curved and higher than it really is.

The craftsmen of yesteryear were frequently guided by a rigid set of rules, measured proportions, and colorations. The Italian Renaissance treatise *Il Libro dell'arte,* written by Florentine painter Cennino Cennini about 1400, affords a glimpse of the training and skills that artists such as Michelangelo were required to master. As a

The height of the renaissance revival of ancient craftsmanship peaked during the Rococo period. This painted ceiling has been created using the trompe-l'oeil *technique.*

*One
of the craftsmen of Biltmore, Campbell,
Smith Reproductions, engaged in the
delicate and precise work of hand-
painted motifs (above).*

boy, Michelangelo served many hard and rigorous years as an apprentice under a very dictatorial master. He spent the long years between boyhood and manhood developing the technique and style for which he would later become famous. Understanding this makes his unique achievement in the Sistine Chapel even more remarkable. During the 1500s, the Italians also began making marblized papers that they could glue onto walls. Wainscoting, crown moldings, and richly colored ceilings soon became preferable to the hanging tapestries, leathers, and silk fabrics that had been much in vogue up to that time. These and other Italian decorative tastes heavily influenced French court art, along with bas-relief stucco designs, decorative wall and ceiling paintings, stenciling, and painted borders and friezes.

As the middle class flourished in Renaissance Italy, the feudal system began to collapse in northern Europe. The French kings, interested in establishing colonies in Italy, lost their campaigns to establish a foothold and, by 1530, the techniques and styles of Italian artisans had gained prominence over the French instead. Three French kings—Francis II, Charles IX, and Henry III—were the sons of an Italian woman, Catherine de' Medici of Florence. Not surprisingly, by the end of their reigns, the court architecture and ornamentation in France was completely Italian in manner, style, and scale.

Even though the Italian craftsmen and their art gained prominence in France, the English were reluctant to adopt the style that is now known as French Classic Revival. Instead, they adopted the ideas of the Dutch Renaissance movement. The Dutch continued to affect the development of English decorative arts primarily because their art was more in sympathy with the nature-loving Celtic heritage that formed the traditional taste of Britain.

Handpainted wallcoverings began to come into vogue after French merchants, on one of their voyages to India in the late 1600s, learned the secrets of Indian fabric printing and established facilities in France to make hand-stamped fabrics. These fabrics were hung on walls as a part of the interior design scheme, and led to the development of hand-printed wallpapers used for the same purpose. The English, too, expanded their international trade, and the Eastern influence in painted decorative arts continued in Britain for some time to come.

English styles changed little, however, from the time of the reign of Queen Mary until the 1800s. Both Queen Mary and, later, Queen Anne were domestic monarchs who created their own hand-painted floral motifs on wood panels using artistic styles that reflected the English taste for nature. These painted wood panels were popular at the time, as were other hand-painted heraldic ornamental decorations on walls and ceiling beams.

During the reigns of George I and George II, interior designers such as Isaac Ware, Abraham Swan, and Thomas Johnson, as well as craftsmen who worked with decorative ornamentalists such as Edwards and Darley, Ince and Mayhew, Mainwaring, W. and J. Halfpenny, all began developing rich wall treatments with exotic designs, gilded leathers, handpainted stippled walls, and other treatments. During the seventeenth and eighteenth centuries, the decorative art of Europe and Italy reflected a Chinese influence, as Chinese craftsmen were imported and the pavilion-type of architecture began to spring forth. The panel inserts on the walls of chateaus and English country houses were filled with Chinese paintings of European themes.

During the eighteenth century, the expansion of the painted decorative arts, now firmly established in England by craftsmen under the direction of Scottish architect Robert Adam, also continued. Adam was, in part, inspired by the decorated tombs of the Etruscans and the tomb of Vulci in Italy. The latter displayed the ancient technique of lining a tomb with a stucco facing and then painting it to simulate marble. Adam was also influenced by the rooms in the tombs that had walls painted delicately with reds, yellows, blues, black, and white, in scenes that depicted the possessions of the owner of the tomb. In his own designs for what would become the creation of some of the most exquisite rooms in English manor houses, Adam was careful to use the classic formula of proportions and colorations. He was so successful that this period of grand style architecture is now often referred to as the Adam Period.

Many of the art styles of England and Europe made up the major decorative influences that were carried to the North American colonies. The English Gothic, William and Mary, Queen Anne, and Georgian painted art forms were simplified by the colonists to represent the more domestically bold art of the early American immigrants, now referred to as Colonial, Williamsburg, and Pennsylvania Dutch.

Painted decorative arts were slow to develop in the colonies, but by the time of the French and Indian wars, Georgian architectural and painted decorative styles had become well established in many Eastern Seaboard cities. As a rule, the same garden scenes that were painted on the walls of many early American homes appeared in English homes, and a simple-patterned wallpaper had begun to be made and installed. The Classical Revival styles of William and Mary, Queen Anne, George I, and

George II were simplified and made in local materials. In the southern states, the Mississippi Valley, and the central region of Canada, French styles prevailed until the fall of Napoleon Bonaparte.

The colonies suffered from a critical shortage of supplies during this time, however, and colonists who ordered paint powders and wallpapers from Europe waited at least a year for their materials. If a colonist traveled to Europe for any reason, on his return trip he carried any wallpaper or paint powders that he might need for decorative projects.

Meanwhile, in Europe, expanded trade with the Orient began to stimulate the growing English middle class as well as the gentry. Trade was especially brisk in hand-painted papers and silks from China and Japan. Marble-ized wallpapers from Italy were also being imported. By the 1800s, European and British homeowners were adorning their walls and ceilings with gilding, silver foiling, handpainted wallpapers, silks, canvases, and the like, all in rich, exotic colors.

English tastes enjoyed worldwide popularity during the Victorian Age, when stencil art and hand-printed and -stenciled wallpapers replaced the more traditional and expensive murals that had decorated the walls before that time. Some "modern" architects of England also used hand-stenciled friezes along the upperwall section at the ceiling. Paneling was usually limited to wainscot, while hand-blocked and -printed patterned wallpaper was often used to decorate walls with elaborate designs.

The Machine Age of the 1900s, however, replaced the elegance, care, and integrity of finely painted ornamentation with the newly discovered expedience of mass production and modernization. Hand craftsmanship was pushed into the background of interior design.

© Grace Davies/Envision

A
hand-painted border between painted ceiling moldings and stained door surrounds is just enough to bring the upper regions of this room alive (above).

*B*efore
wallpaper was introduced in Europe in the eighteenth century, walls were stenciled with repeat patterns. Here, Oriental floral motifs have been used to create a special wall treatment (left).

© E. Silva/FPG International

Bradbury and Bradbury created the handmade wallpapers and ceiling treatments in this room (near right). Classic colors, motifs, and detailed molding carefully proportioned to the size of the room all work together to provide a pleasing period decor.

Combining several handmade wallpapers to cover every inch of wall was a popular Victorian concept (hand-screened by Bradbury and Bradbury, far right, above). The careful choice of historic colors and motifs makes the combination work successfully.

The advent of sameness caused by the Machine Age inspired a return to craftsmanship in the late nineteenth century. Here is a handmade border paper after the manner of the designer, William Morris (handmade by Bradbury and Bradbury, far right, bottom).

Courtesy Bradbury & Bradbury Wallpapers/© Ron Mitchell

BRUCE BRADBURY

Making the finest of nineteenth century arts and crafts to suit the integrity of not only original designs, but also those that incorporate contemporary tastes, has been de rigeur for artist designer Bruce Bradbury for many years.

Giving in to his lifelong fascination with Victoriana, Bradbury traveled to England as a young man, where he studied the extensive wallpaper collection at the renowned Victoria and Albert Museum. He followed that with study at the William Morris Museum (also in England), then returned to the States to apprentice at two different wallpaper manufacturers. Ultimately, Bradbury founded Bradbury and Bradbury, one of the few studios that only creates wallpapers of nineteenth century designs with authentic techniques, with each color band mixed and silkscreened onto the wallpaper, one painstaking color at a time.

Recognizing a pronounced return to a love of pattern and color today, Bradbury is enthusiastic about the rebirth of wallpaper as one of the great ornamental styles of artistic interior design. Since the Victorian era was the heyday of wallpaper, Bradbury has sought to match the exuberance of that period by providing over 100 different nineteenth-century handcrafted wallpaper designs. While many of these designs are authentic, museum-quality recreations of the originals, often done in the Morris tradition, Bradbury also creates original designs that convey the artistic impact of the period. The results are breathtaking backdrops in a style that Bradbury calls Victorian Revival.

Considered an expert on Victoriana, Bradbury lectures extensively on decorative wall and ceiling treatments to all who care to listen and learn. He is ever alert to new revelations about the Victorian era and is in touch with 20,000 owners of Victorian houses who, along with his other sources, provide a wealth of information on the subject.

George Lucas, producer of Star Wars, *commissioned Bradbury to do a design study of the wallpaper that Queen Victoria had in her throne room in St. James Palace. Bradbury's authentic wallpaper designs are currently found in the Government House in Baltimore, Maryland; the Legislative Chambers in New Brunswick, Canada; President Taft's house in Cincinnati, Ohio; and Henry Firestone's simple farmhouse in Greenfield Village, Michigan.*

T rompe l'oeil, _or architectural dimensional painting, dates as far back as the ancient Egyptians and was passed to modern man by the Renaissance Italians. Here, artisans have used this fool-the-eye technique to visually extend the interior space into an English Garden (right)._

Trompe L'oeil

Trompe l'oeil is a special painting technique that was originally developed by the Italians. They wished to extend existing architectural decorations onto a flat surface where they did not actually exist, or to bring the outdoors inside by painting garden scenes on the walls and clouds on the ceilings. Trompe l'oeil should not be confused with fine art canvas painting, nor with mural painting, both of which employ other techniques. Trompe l'oeil techniques use pigment washes over a colored ground. The Venetians, and especially Italian artist Michelangelo, are well known for this technique, but it is probably the French artist Fragonard who is best known for trompe l'oeil mural creations. To create his garden scenes, Fragonard usually worked many layers of oil paint washes over a ground of creamy gray.

The trompe l'oeil specialists of bygone years normally painted their larger creations on seamless canvas. Once the entire scene was finished, the canvas was anchored to the plaster wall or ceiling surface with gesso. This is still done for many larger creations involving trompe l'oeil. Also, today, acrylic paints are often used instead of oil, for the many layers of the mural dry faster. However, these paints do not have the subtle quality of oil paints.

Today, trompe l'oeil is still an art that cannot be executed without substantial artistic training. Also, few trompe l'oeil painters find much regular call for their craft. An exception is in the television, movie, and advertising industries, where craftspeople with trompe l'oeil skills are required in setmaking.

Because of the training required, it can be difficult to apply budgetary restrictions to a trompe l'oeil project. Reducing the scale of the project may be the only real option available if financial corners need to be cut. Take care to select a craftsperson who understands color and scale, who has experience with trompe l'oeil, and can execute the style you want, be it whimsical or classical.

*A*lthough
the corner of this ceiling appears to
feature three-dimensional plaster relief,
it is actually a trompe l'oeil design with
hand-applied gold leaf (above).

*P*aint,
when applied by a knowledgeable
craftsperson, can make almost any
surface appear to be some other
material. This fireplace, hand-painted
by artisans from Evergreene, illustrates
the stunning effect of antiquing, a
process that involves the application of
different-colored glazes over paint.

Exotic
and rare woods were often simulated
with paint by Colonial and Victorian
craftsmen. Here, artisans from
Evergreene have painted wood grains
that are almost indistinguishable from
the real thing (below).

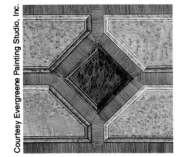

Wood Graining

The trompe l'oeil specialty glazing technique of hand-replicating exotic and costly wood grains was popular from the seventeenth and eighteenth centuries through the Victorian and Art Deco periods in England, Canada, and the United States. Many pine-paneled rooms, especially in Victorian rooms, were painted in this manner to give the appearance of some other, more expensive wood, such as mahogany. During the Art Deco period, this technique was used to simulate rare and exotic woods such as satinwood, zebrawood, and tulipwood.

An age old art form, wood graining is accomplished in the same manner today as it was times past. First, the surface is painted with a prime coat of a gray buff. This coating, which is allowed to dry completely, is then painted with a thick glaze coat of brown in a chosen shade. While the brown glaze coat is still wet, a large graining comb is passed over the surface to push the glaze off of the base coat and create the effect of large veins of the wood. A smaller graining comb is then passed over the surface, and then a brush is used to "fan" the lines and veins that were created by the graining combs. Finally, a thin glaze coating, lightly tinted with umber or brown, is usually applied.

Extensive artistic and technical training is required to accurately replicate real woods and, because of this, wood graining is not generally considered a project that can be undertaken by the nonprofessional. For those who are not concerned with artistic quality or exact replication, simulated wood graining kits, complete with materials, are generally available at the local hardware, household supply, or building supply store. If authentic craftsmanship is important for the project, however, ensure that the craftsperson selected has a background in these wood-graining techniques, and that his or her past projects include the type of wood graining you desire for your project. Budgeting can be difficult, if not impossible, since the time and cost requirements of wood graining can approach the cost of a veneer treatment in the wood required for the project.

Marbleizing

Similar to wood graining, marbleizing is a painting technique that creates the look of marble or granite on plaster, wood, or some other surface. Marbleizing uses many of the same tools and techniques that are used in wood graining, but the difference between the two crafts is that, while trees have similar growth patterns and therefore have like patterns to copy, marble and granite patterns vary greatly and can change significantly in color and pattern. Those differences in pattern need to be taken into account during the replication process.

To marbleize, the surface is prepared by applying a base coat in a color such as gray, green, or black (depending on the stone that is to be replicated). A semitransparent second coat of paint is applied with a special wooden craft stick, waddle, or spongee, depending on the desired pattern. This second coat is always applied in a dribbled or uneven pattern. After this coat is dry, a third tinted coat is applied. This is also a mottled coating that is partially removed with a waddle or dauber made of crumpled paper. The crumpled paper is daubed over the wet surface. At this point, the detailing usually begins with the application of the first layer of veining. Finally, another tinted layer of veining is applied with a brush, normally of a dark and a light color complementary to the colors already used. This layer is worked into the design until the veining process is completed.

The marbleizing process has not really changed over the years, but paint technology has changed drastically. Earlier craftsmen used oil-pigmented paints that had a better capacity for duplicating the translucent quality of polished stone. Today, it is more cost effective to use the readily available acrylic paints, which, although quite

Marbleizing techniques can be used to approximate any of a countless number of actual marbles. This marble pattern was created by John Canning (left).

acceptable, are not really the same as the original oils. The acrylics can be thinned with an acrylic varnish to make the glaze coatings, and most homeowners will find the effect of this adequate. However, acrylic paints will never approximate the quality or the deep color of marbleized wainscots or the marbleized bottoms of old, enameled Victorian bathtubs.

Budgeting for marbleizing generally involves scale and pattern. If funds are limited, restrict the area to some trim work or one focal point for interest. Selecting a simple stone pattern rather than a more complex pattern, also makes a difference. The more complicated the pattern, the more steps and, therefore, time and talent is required from the craftsperson. If it is a flat surface that is to be marbleized, a craftsperson might be able, at a lesser fee, to execute the design at his/her studio (rather than on site), and then apply it to your surface.

As with other painted crafts, in marbleizing, experience counts. While the more simple patterns, such as white marble, can be replicated with some success by craftspeople with less training and experience, the more complicated patterns of, for example, Rouge Royal, Vert de Mer, or Oriental Verdantique generally require the hand of a person who has a good technical education. An exception to this might be a project that includes folk art decoration, which is more whimsical and relaxed, and therefore a bit easier to execute. In any case, a craftsperson who has marbleized in the different patterns, and especially in a pattern similar to what is required for the project, is most likely the best person for the job.

This neoclassic stenciled pattern creates a stunning focal point in any room design. The subtle colors also combine well with wood moldings (hand-stenciled wallpaper frieze by Evergreene; above).

Stencil Art

Stencil art is the same today as it was during the yesteryear, except that, again, the paints used have changed dramatically. During the Victorian period, most stencil artists traveled from city to city with dry paint powders that they mixed with a base such as milk or turpentine and linseed oil at the site. This paint mixture was then applied through a precut stencil with a brush that is very similar to a shaving brush. The colors were normally applied through the stencil so that they were not solid, but varied in intensity to provide a variety in hue that added interest and elegance. Today's acrylic paints tend to be less transparent and more synthetic in color tone.

Authentic style stencil patterns are still available today, and some companies still have precut stencils and color keys that faithfully reproduce those from the nineteenth century. The colored frieze patterns and borders that were popularized by Englishman William Morris during the Arts and Crafts Movement in the late 1800s are still reproduced by some companies with authentic style techniques and color tones. While stenciling may look simple, the technical expertise required can be more than one realizes. Laying the pattern properly, executing straight lines (particularly when there is more than one line), and selecting a proper color palette are all aspects of stenciling that normally cannot be undertaken with success by the nonprofessional or even the art student. In any project, the level of expertise required should dictate the selection of the craftsperson. A person with less training and experience, such as the average art student, does not have adequate technical skill to complete the more complicated patterns and colorations of the stencil arts. However, an art student might be able to execute the simpler styles, such as Pennsylvania Dutch or the simple Gothic or classic border patterns, that are classified as folk art. Budget considerations can be accommodated by avoiding complex patterns and limiting the number of colors selected for the project.

Phillip Gould/Stock Options

Courtesy Larry Boyce & Assoc./Gatewood Residence

*T*his
neoclassic ceiling, with band-stencilled and hand-painted insets, was created by modern day artisans from Larry Boyce & Associates (above).

*T*his
band-painted and stencilled-art ceiling is a Victorian adaptation of classical motifs. The centre ceiling medallion is of a French influence, while the border is an English trellis pattern (left).

JOHN CANNING

Dedicated to a personalized approach, John Canning specializes in ornamental painting and church decoration in the tradition of the British craftsmen. At an early age, Canning began his studies at the Scottish Decorative Trades Institute and the Stow College of Building in Glasgow, Scotland. When he was only nineteen, he earned a London City and Guilds Certificate after serving a five-year apprenticeship in ornamental painting and decorating.

Trompe l'oeil, stenciling, marbleizing, and wood graining are but some of the artistic crafts that Canning has mastered over the years. His firm, John Canning & Co., established in Connecticut in 1976, practices these and other traditional painting techniques. The company is proficient in designs of the eighteenth century, Art Nouveau, and Art Deco periods, but has a special expertise in Victorian decoration as exemplified by the Aesthetic Movement.

Although Canning is frequently called upon for custom design work, much of his work comes from restoration. He emphasizes the importance of accurate historical information on any project, but, convinced that the dogmatic attitude that often accompanies preservation efforts doesn't always work, Canning works with a counsel of several experts. He believes that interpretation is relative and that teamwork is the answer to accuracy in a replication or restoration project.

Canning claims that people became brainwashed by Bauhaus, and he is delighted at the current revival of the beauty and color of authentic craftsmanship. He is particularly inspired by the techniques and styles that were popular and done with such exacting standards during the Victorian era. Following the example of many of the artists of that period, he has mastered the arts of free-hand work, shading, and striping that are often such an integral part of the overall design in stenciling; his wood-graining talents are matched by few people today. He acknowledges marbleizing as an opportunity for expression, and his trompe l'oeil talents are extraordinary.

Canning's work can be seen in the Sterling Library, the Battell Chapel at Yale University, and Connecticut State's Senate Chambers, House of Representatives, and Hall of Flags. Canning's unique residential interiors have included a combination of trompe l'oeil and other techniques to exactly replicate the motifs of the Rothschild china for a centerpiece on a dining room floor, and wood-graining techniques to match several different grades of wood to the original woods throughout an authentic Victorian home. Ironically, Canning himself lives in a modern split-level home, but he has converted his garage into a fully executed Art Nouveau room, which he calls the McIntosh Room.

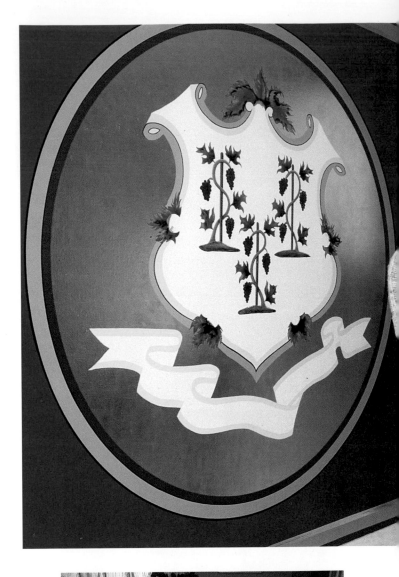

*C*raftsman
*John Canning is here in the process of
creating this historic heraldric
wall painting (above).*

*J*ohn
*Canning used marbleizing, pickling,
combing, and stenciling techniques to
create the design treatments on the
floor of this room (left).*

*T*he
*rug pattern with one corner turned up
is painted directly onto the wood floor
(right).*

*L*incrusta
*and Anaglypta are embossed paper
products that can be used to create
raised friezes (above bottom). The
texture pattern that imprints the paper
is engraved onto brass rollers (above
top), many of which date back to
Victorian times.*

*H*and-stamping
*techniques used to create repeated
patterns on wallpaper originated in
India and were adapted by England
and France. Today, these papers are
being faithfully reproduced for use in
modern, as well as historic, homes
(right).*

Wallpapers

Handpainted and hand-screened wallpapers originated in China and India. In sixteenth century Italy, the Domini Papers—small marbleized sheets that were arranged in patterns on the wall—were popular. By 1710, handpainted papers were being imported to Europe from China, and fabric-stamping methods were being adapted to papers in France. In Italy, in the 1700s, a wallcovering was introduced that consisted of a canvas painted with a dull gold, then stenciled with two-toned damask patterns with different shadings of color so that some areas were quite transparent. This wallcovering was eventually revived and made famous by the Fortuni family. Japanese papers of gold and silver with hand-decorated designs had become popular in Europe by the late 1700s as well. Eventually, the French and English began making paneled papers to be applied in sequence to depict scenes of hunting excursions, exotic ports of India, and the like.

Stripes, dots, diamonds, and other patterns were also being stamped out in the Indian technique, which used hand-carved wood blocks. These imported, handpainted papers, as well as the scenic panel papers that were expensive even when first created, were normally carefully removed from the walls of rooms being redecorated and resold. Today, there are still some dealers who trade in antique, handpainted wallpapers.

The introduction of machine printing during the Victorian period ushered in the heyday of wallpaper design. By the late 1800s, a parlor room could easily feature twelve to fifteen different-patterned wallpapers.

"Machine" printing was done with huge pearwood blocks that had been carved by hand, a different block for each color in the design that would be on the paper. These blocks were then placed onto a huge felt pad that had been soaked with a flat oil paint, and then "stamped" on the paper. This process was repeated for each color in the design.

Today, this process is duplicated with silkscreening instead of blocks. A large wooden frame is constructed, across which a piece of fabric is tightly stretched. A design is handpainted onto a mylar surface and then, through a photographic process, transferred onto the fabric or silkscreen, where the design pattern takes on a stencillike texture. The screen is then lined up and registered (aligned), laid down on the paper, then paint is poured into the frame. A large rubber squeegee is used to pull the color across and through the fabric, transferring the design onto the wallpaper. This process is repeated for each color in each pattern. Today, the wallpaper for an average-size room could require as many as four to five thousand strokes, with each one being registered and pulled by hand.

There are still some craftspeople who use this process to print period wallpapers, borders, and friezes, or to create authentic designs that incorporate the old with the new. It is impossible for the nonprofessional to execute this special technique, but the papers can be ordered from the studios that make them. Some replicated wallpaper designs are more authentically styled than others, with color, quality, pattern, and historic accuracy often determining the price. A wallpaper that is not done by hand, but still has the look of the period of your project, may be the answer if there are budget concerns. Or, you can paint your walls a solid color and paper the ceiling with a handpainted paper, creating dramatic impact for a lower cost. Simply installing a hand-printed frieze or border papers will also create a nice effect on a lower budget.

Many wallpapers can be ordered pretrimmed. Patterns need to be matched during installation, and often this is best done by a professional; most studios provide this service. The walls need to be specially cleaned and prepared before the wallpaper is applied, and the paper must be laid on the wall in such a way that bubbles do not set in between the wall and the paper. Most wallpapers, whether ordered through a standard retail outlet or a studio, will come with some installation instructions, but unless you are handy, it is best to leave this to the installation service provided by the shop or studio that sells you the paper.

The hand-painted wallpaper in a soft duo-tone brings a sense of presence to this hallway (below). The thin molding, plain painted border, and darker colored ceiling treatment complement the pattern in the paper. This is a creative way to carry out a coherent design scheme without great expense.

© C. Schneider/FPG International

STONE AND MARBLE

The Stone Age marked the beginnings of the stonecarver's craft. Over the centuries, stonecarvers have developed their knowledge and skills to use stone in a functional as well as a decorative manner. While the earliest stone housing predates 6000 B.C. in the Indus Valley, it was the Egyptians who introduced Western man to the benefits and grace of stone.

The Egyptians developed a technology for transporting huge stone blocks on fragile barges. They refined methods of leverage, hoisting, and cutting, making the design and construction of the pyramids possible. They used slaves to cut the stone from the rock quarries (the extreme hardship and high death rate of the quarry workers is well known). Hard physical labor was required to chip the stone away from the mountainside with hand tools with serated blades and hammers and chisels. The fine dust created during the stonecutting process penetrated the workers' lungs,

This detail of a purple-veined marble fireplace exemplifies the richness afforded by a simple stone carving (near right).

Doorway surrounds and pediments have been created from carved stone since early times. Today's craftspeople are often called upon to recreate doorways, such as this Gothic doorway at St. Anne's Church in Houston, Texas (far right).

Almost everyone dreams of one day luxuriating in a pink marble bathroom. This example is particularly enticing because of the beautiful craftsmanship of the marble floor, tub, and fireplace (previous page).

© Grace Davies/Envision

virtually guaranteeing them an early death.

This labor force of slaves helped Egypt grow architecturally, through the dynasties of Ahknaten and Ramses. A basic stone temple evolved that consisted of a rectangular stone building with a flat roof and, usually, a row of columns in the front.

This design was eventually adopted by the Greeks and ultimately handed down to contemporary man. With stone more plentiful than wood, Greeks during their Golden Age found stone the building material of choice, and as the Greek culture prospered, so did the stonecutters. The Greeks built temples that the stonecarvers carved with relief work symbolizing the growing power, strength, and wealth of the culture. The Greeks continued their love affair with stone, carving statuary and other architectural details with outstanding realism and incomparable proportions. They often painted and inlaid the stone with ivory, ebony, bronze, or gold, and inset colored stone and marble into the floors and wainscot panels in geometric patterns to provide beautiful backgrounds for otherwise sparsely furnished rooms.

The Greek craftsmen of this period were intensely dedicated to their craft and made great advances in technique. Along with a sense of proportion, the Greek stonecutters of this period added scientific observation to their

craft. They detailed the characteristics of the object being sculpted—leaf, lion, vine, flower, woman. A repertoire of foliations was augmented with stylized geometric diaper designs. Exterior cornice courses and roof eave decorations were carefully developed to add protection against the rain. Eave soffit edges and molding overhangs were deliberately shaped and slanted so that rain would run off and away from the building facade instead of creeping into the building walls. Rosette coffers were cut into soffit eaves with artfully designed animals and foliations, creating additional projections that would keep the water out.

Many of these ideas were quickly adapted by the Romans, and the techniques used in stonecarving did not change for many years. As the western Roman Empire fell, the Byzantine Empire (the eastern part of the Roman Empire) prospered and continued to develop. During this time, the Christian art styles of the Byzantine Empire were also growing, encouraged by the Church's support of the development of art and architecture. Craftsmen of the Byzantine culture reintroduced vaulted arches that had originally been developed by the bricklayers of Mesopotamia around 4000 B.C. They also developed heavy support columns that allowed the roof weight of their structures to be increased. The style of building that used both of these elements eventually influenced the Gothic architectural style later established in Europe.

It was the stone masons of Europe who eventually solved the problem of roof weight caused by the added height of the vaulted ceilings. Flying buttresses were added to the exterior of buildings during the Gothic period to ensure the soundness and integrity of the structure. The flying buttress, vaulted ceilings, arches, and Gothic traceries provided the background for a cornucopia of carved stone designs that were mixed in a unique way. The architectural details of these carved stone elements included gargoyles, demons, and other mythic beings, as well as the naturalistic foliations on corbels, capitals, cornices, frieze panels, and entablatures. Foliage carvings and diaper designs were stacked one on top of the other. All of this was combined to create a rhythm of design that, in the filtered light of these lofty spaces, seemed to move about the room.

During the Middle Ages, the towns and villages throughout Europe grew into communities. People banded together for mutual protection. Cities were walled, and therefore did not provide adequate space for large private quarters. The abbot, the lord, and his court and their households occupied the main buildings, and the great hall and marketplace were the center of daily life for all members of the community. Inside the castle or home, the fireplace was the central feature, serving to ward off the damp and cold that permeated the stone walls and floors. In peasants' homes, the ceilings were kept low, so the rooms would be easy to heat.

In the great hall, the fireplace was often gigantic, and it provided the only source of heat and served as the cooking facility. The stonecutter and mason who could construct a fireplace that drew correctly and did not belch smoke was in great demand. Besides mastering the engineering problems created by the height of these stone structures, these artisans also experimented with the fitting of stone and stone joinery. The techniques developed during this period were later combined with a revival of classic styles.

Although the Middle Ages were a harsh time when most people did not live in comfort, their faith and expression of hope persevered. In the later periods of Gothic construction, cathedrals became a perfect reflection of the stonecarver's art. The stonecarver freely added grotesque animals and beings to his designs to express the belief that good triumphed over evil. Although the ideas and concepts of the Gothic stonecarvers were sometimes different and special motifs were featured from place to place, they still used the same mallets, hammers, chisels, and scrapers as the earlier artisans.

The fireplace traditionally occupied a place of great importance in historical residences. This French Empire fireplace incorporates both ancient Roman and Egyptian motifs into its design.

While the ideas of Renaissance Classic Revivalism surfaced in England under Henry VIII, it was not until the seventeenth century that the English fully adapted the grand scale and ornamentation of classic design. The famous British adventurer and designer Inigo Jones and his peers became enamored with the principles of design that had been established by the Italian Renaissance architect, Palladio in the Mid 1500's. As a result, the Palladian styles (based on Italian Classic designs) began to appear in England.

By the mid 1800s, the Palladian (Baroque) styles were firmly established in England. The British Adam brothers rose to prominence as the leading designers of the day. Craftsmanship was precise and the training demanding. Marble features often dominated the formal rooms of English homes. The marble grand staircase, entry floors, fluted pilasters, and the appropriate capitals, cornices, and moldings were lavishly displayed. The door entablature and surrounds were often fitted with symmetrically balanced pediments of several types—straight, canted, or curvilinear. An urn or bust carved from stone was often placed in the center. Doorways, windows, and mantels were an important part of the room arrangement. The Adam brothers preferred pure white, finely carved marble mantels with urns, garlands, drops, low relief figures, and fluting, and they were sometimes inset with colored Italian marbles in buff, yellow, black, and green tones. Fireplace screens and andirons were coordinated with the mantel and mantel surrounds to complete the look.

In the colonies, the Palladian styles were adapted to a somewhat more simplified scale. Also adapted was a graceful French style, referred to as Louis Seize or French Provincial, that was developed in France after the French Revolution and was a more domestic and comfortable interpretation of the French Classic styles. Although many of the French and English fireplaces, door pediments, and staircases in the colonies were copied in wood, the scaled-down carved marble or stone mantel was also used and became a status symbol for its beauty and elegance.

As peace began to slowly settle over Europe, country estates with stone walls, floors, and fireplaces came into favor. The Georgian period brought an increase in the status of stone and marble in England, and, consequently, in the New World, as European aristocrats began financing plantations and other enterprises on the American continent. These structures featured formal areas and halls made from marble and other favored stones. The floors, walls, or wainscots were often highlighted with stone columns and carved capitals. The stone floors and walls would often be enriched with inlay, displaying the status and wealth of the owner. Floors were frequently composed of specially shaped stone tiles cut from different colors and types of stone, artfully laid into geometric patterns. Wainscots were inlaid with colored stone, with the Greek diamond serving as a favorite motif.

Meanwhile, the rural areas were also built up with stone. As farmers moved away from village centers to work the land, they frequently constructed their houses with the rocks that were gathered during the clearing of the land. At the same time in the cities, brick became a major building material, and the demand for stonecutters dwindled. Brick houses were frequently accented only with stone groins (corner pieces), stone entablatures, and window trims. The fireplace mantel had become a detached, movable piece of furniture, and was significantly scaled down from earlier periods. Stone mantels remained a main feature, but more often than not, these were being carved in workshops and shipped to the project.

The famous French queen, Marie Antoinette, commissioned a special room with decorated cabinetry to use for toiletry that set a precedent for the ornamentation of the bathroom that influenced the designers and craftsmen of the late 1800s. Then the invention of plumbing, toilets, and the fixed bathtub opened new possibilities for the bathroom. This room was a new luxury, out of financial reach for the common man, but quickly adopted by the

wealthy. The most lavish and costly trimmings were used as decorations, and special furniture was designed to hold perfumes and other toiletry items. Marble enclosed the tub and toilet and was also used for flooring and wainscots. Sometimes, handcarved *boisserie* paneling was combined with marble and glazed tile to decorate the room. The porcelain commode featured handpainted decorations that were as fine as the designs found on dinnerware. During the Victorian period—as the bathroom became popular and available, finally, to the middle class—marbleized patterns were painted onto bathtubs and wooden wainscots.

The Victorian Age signaled the end of the use of stone and marble for architectural ornamentation. Advancing industrialization caused stoneworkers to gather in collective workshops, where modern equipment was developed for cutting and polishing marble and stone. Today, stonecutting equipment includes specially made saws that are fitted with blades coated with diamond dust, that use water as a lubricant and cut through the hardest granite. Huge polishing wheels and power tools fitted with grinders of every size chip away and grind down marble and stone. Special drills are used to add incised decoration. Modern casting compounds are mixed with powdered marble dust and used to produce faux marble. This method and compound is also used to make repairs and replace chips of broken and damaged marble artifacts.

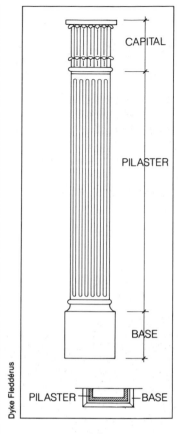

*T*be fluted pilaster of Georgian England reflects its origins in the classical Roman Corinthian style. The proportion of the column height, base, and capitol is based on the maximum width of the column itself.

*T*his lavish bathroom with marble appointments suits contemporary lifestyles while reflecting a French Art Deco influence (left).

ALLEN WILLIAMS

© Tony Cenicola

Like so many other craftspeople, Allen Williams grew up around what was to become his trade. He completed his first stone carving at the age of nine under the watchful eyes of his father, who had worked the stone quarries since the 1930s. Later, Williams took a trip to Ireland and England, where he spent time talking to architectural as well as letter carvers. In 1972, he took over his father's business, Chester Granite, in Blandford, Massachusetts.

Chester Granite's carvers work with granite, brownstone, slate, marble, and limestone to provide restoration and custom designs through relief carving, architectural carving, lettering, and hand dressing. Their hand-lettering work is called upon for cemetery work, cornerstones, memorials, and friezes with inscriptions. The hand-dressing required for stone doorways, windowsills, steps, and the like is a specialty at Chester Granite, where they still use authentic hand tools to do the job. Williams's favorite craft, relief carving, is applied to a full range of projects, from mantels to statuary.

The basic saw cuts at Chester Granite are done by machine, with air-powered chisels also used for granite. All other work is done by hand, with a mallet and chisel. For restoration projects, Williams, who has studied the history of stone-carving in the Northeastern United States, always tries to get replacement stone from the quarry where it was originally worked. If the quarry no longer exists, he tries to locate the stone that originated in that quarry in a salvage yard.

Williams considers the job he is working on at any given time to be the most interesting one. Notably, he carved the memorials that were used for the opening scenes in the movie Ironweed. *Other work at Chester Granite covers a full spectrum of projects, from work on an 1860s granite church to the replacement of carved stonework for the Memorial Hall at Harvard University in Cambridge, Massachusetts.*

Courtesy Chester Granite

Courtesy Chester Granite

*A*llen
Williams uses the stone mason's tools in
the same way that his predecessors did
for centuries (above left). Notice the
vacuum in the background, which
makes his job much easier without
compromising his craftsmanship.

*T*he
ancient art and precision of stone
carving has been revived by Allen
Williams at Chester Granite Co., to
create this timely masterpiece
(below left).

© Tony Cenicola

© Maria Pape

Restoration Guidelines

One technique used today for stone decoration is etching stone with sandblasting equipment or caustic acids. This was perfected during the Art Deco period and is used especially for shallow-cut surface ornamentation. The desired design is masked off with a resistant material and either blasted with a stream of fine sand grit or bathed in a solution of acid. This acid or sand grit attacks the stone or marble and eats away the unprotected areas, creating the design.

Honed surfaces, which resemble hand-chiseled surfaces, can also be achieved by a chemical process. After the stone or marble is cut, the surface is treated with special chemicals that attack the weaker areas of the crystal bonds, which causes the weakened areas to flake away from the stone surface. Use of these chemicals and methods requires special knowledge as well as safe procedures and should not be attempted without proper training, equipment, and supervision.

Modern conservation techniques have been developed to clean and restore marble. Marble and stone are actually brittle, porous crystalline formations. Often, various minerals, such as iron, are present in the stone and can eventually cause stains. Atmospheric pollutants, such as sulfur dioxide, cigarette smoke, industrial smoke, and dust all tend to settle into the stone pores, which results in a buildup of dirt on the surface. A patina begins to build, leading to the first stages of stone deterioration. Once the pores of the marble (or stone) have become clogged, a simple washing will not remove the dirt. If the pores of a marble floor become clogged with wax, for instance, marble fatigue can result. The earliest sign of this deterioration in polished surfaces is when the surface begins to crystallize and form a patina. Marble flooring with irregular holes and chips is an example of stone in the advanced stages of fatigue. Because of this, marble flooring should be properly treated with special marble sealers and waxes.

Once a piece of marble has been chipped, it cannot easily be restored and often must be replaced altogether. You will need to contact a restoration specialist to consider the options available to you. Special compounds that are mixed with marble have been formulated to be used to repair and remodel broken areas of marble. Successful applications of these compounds is virtually impossible when attempted by an amateur, and because of this, working with a professional is virtually the only solution to a problem of this nature.

Several prestigious museums and universities, as well as many commercial companies have pioneered the research and development of stone cleaning processes, sealers, and waxes. Most museums and universities do not provide direct services for restoring and cleaning marble. However, they might be able to refer you to a conservator or specialist. Students are not generally qualified to do stone and marble restoration work, so coordination with a professional is, without a doubt, the best way to approach the problem. Cleaning should also be executed by a professional, since some cleaning procedures can exacerbate present deterioration or cause additional damage if improperly performed by unskilled and inexperienced hands.

Some cleaning, waxing, and sealing can be done by the homeowner. Most large marble suppliers carry the necessary cleaning compounds and sell sealers and waxes that have been pretested by building materials conservators and commercial institutions. Special poultice compounds containing magnesium and clay are used to clean the dirt and grime from the pores of the stone and marble. Polishes have been developed specifically for marble that do not clog the pores, but allow the stone to "breathe" while providing a water seal. Regular paste

A
marble fireplace features sphinxlike carvings that reflect the Egyptian influence in French Empire designs (above).

This
grandiose design demonstrates some cost-saving possibilities when working with marble (left). Although the floor is made of marble, the walls and columns are actually painted in a faux marble pattern.

Displaying
another cost effective alternative, this beautiful marble bath with columns is not marble at all, but pigmented resin cast to emulate stone (far left).

Marble

floors contribute dramatic impact to a room. The shine of the polished stone reflects and accentuates the other elements in a room, such as these magnificent staircases (right and far right). Though each room displays a different design theme, note that both recognize that a marble floor, because of its grandeur, requires wide open space.

waxes should never be used as a water sealant.

Marble floors can be maintained by occasionally mopping them with mild soap and water. Any scrubbing should be done with natural bristle brushes only. These same cleaning techniques should be used on marble walls and tub enclosures. The marble, and especially the grout, around tubs and wash basins should be checked periodically. Frequently, the grout between the marble pieces will deteriorate before the marble sealers and waxed surface does. When this occurs, water begins seeping in around the edges of the marble and can slowly damage the marble from underneath. Marble waxes are usually applied with extra fine steel wool and buffed with lambswool pads. Depending on foot traffic, a marble floor may need to be waxed once or twice each year by a professional.

Marble and stonework has always been very expensive. Ancient Romans, and even the Victorian designers, tried to reduce the expense by employing trompe-l'oeil artists to paint surfaces with marbleized patterns. The Victorians constructed a water-tight wainscot around the bathtub which they then painted with a marble pattern. Today, although marbleizing is very expensive, it could very well be less expensive than installing or replacing the stone altogether, so it could help cut costs (see Chapter Two, Paint). Another budgeting idea is to limit the use of stone to the formal areas, such as the entry, or as an accent around the basin in the bathroom. Limiting the use of marble or stone to make an important architectural feature even more outstanding can help keep costs down yet enhance the beauty of the stone within the design.

Finely polished and carved stonework in translucent white marbles, as well as in the beautifully colored marbles, travertines, slates, and granites, have always held a special place in the cultures of the world. Reverence for the richness and dignity of stone has continued unabated throughout the millennia to modern man. Carved stone, properly cared for, will outlive generations to come, providing a long-lasting tribute to the craftsperson's ability to adapt nature to the everyday living sensibilities of homeowners everywhere.

*H*ere
*is a creative and rather unconventional
way to use marble in the home—where
carpet is usually found (above). The
philosophy here is that the marble is
remarkably beautiful, so don't cover it.
Combined with a mix of fabrics and
patterns and complemented by wood,
marble is the perfect floor treatment.*

ALAN BIRD

Englishman Alan Bird claims that he has stone dust in his blood. His connection to stone goes back as far as he can remember. His grandfather, father, and uncle (who worked on Bath Abbey) all worked with stone. As a child in the village of Priddy, near Stonehenge, Bird amused himself with the Roman artifacts that littered the area. He also found stones that could be fashioned into daggers and swords to complement the arrowheads he discovered scattered in the fields separated only by limestone walls.

At the age of fifteen, Bird was accepted as an apprentice stonecutter for Wells Cathedral near Bristol. The first apprentice allowed to work on the Cathedral in twenty years, Bird stayed on for the next thirteen years before moving on to New York to work at the Stoneyard Institute, Incorporated.

Here at the Stoneyard Institute Bird is the master mason who oversees all of the stone cutting for the cathedral project, which, except for the primary cut, is done entirely by hand. All geometrical stone is cut for capitals, quatrefoils, tracery panels, circular bases, doorways, windowsills, and the like. Bird has cut stones for the Villa de la Rosa in Jerusalem, Trinity Church on Wall Street in New York City, and for a tea garden in Japan.

But by far the most important project under Bird's cutting direction is the Cathedral of St. John the Divine in New York City. Begun in 1892, this ongoing project, when completed, will be the largest church in the world except for St. Peter's in Rome. Bird and his staff started cutting for the project in 1979, with the actual building beginning in 1982. To date, thirty two feet of the first tower has been set into place. With 150 feet of stone needed for just one tower, Bird hopes to see one completed, but does not expect to see the entire project finished during his lifetime.

However, Bird's dream of carrying on the vision of the original masons of the Cathedral has already been realized. To help ensure that this dream is continued, Bird passes on his skill and knowledge through an apprenticeship program that draws members of all ages from the surrounding Harlem community. The apprentices learn to carve and set the stone, which complements the cutting techniques that Bird teaches. The program provides the participants, who are members of the community, with the opportunity to carry this craft into the future on behalf of not only the cathedral but of those who care deeply about this dying craft.

Often wondering how his work will be judged hundreds of years from now, Bird exercises patience and diligence in his craft. Striving for perfection, he always gives "100 percent to the craft." The Indiana limestone that he works with is 300 million years old—give or take a million years— and each time he hits it with a chisel, he feels that he is bringing it back to life. It gives him great pleasure and satisfaction to know that the life of that stone, once set into place, will outlast his own life by at least twenty times over.

Courtesy Stoneyard Institute/© Robert F. Rodriguez

Courtesy Stoneyard Institute

On

site at the Cathedral of Saint John the
Divine, the team from the Stoneyard
Institute works on many different areas
of this enormous authentic restoration
at once (left). Above are some of the
mason's tools, used by stone crafters
yesterday and today.

TILE

The art and technology of glazed decorative tiles has a long and important history. Archaeologists have vigorously debated the issue of whose art is the oldest: the Egyptians' or the Mesopotamians' (including the ancient peoples of Ur, Chaldea, and Sumer). There is evidence that by 4000 B.C., the Egyptians were creating blue and white glazed tiles and the Sumerians were creating mosaics. Tiles were used for decoration and as a water sealant in the valley of the Euphrates River, where buildings were made of sun-dried bricks.

Ceramic craftsmanship began with the making of simple containers and eating vessels. The first decorations on these vessels were incisions made with sticks, or other "tooling." The patterns were primitive lines and geometrics. Sun-dried clay tiles were used as roofing materials to keep out rain, and, in later periods, clay troughs and hollow cylinders were used by the early Mesopotamians to direct the flow of water. These beginnings led to the plumbing and

terra cotta roofs of the villas and palaces of the Roman Empire.

Tiles originated with earthenware pottery made from clay that was taken from the ground by hand. The clay was kneaded by villagers called "earth treaders." They stomped the red clay with their feet until the water was equally distributed throughout the clay mass so that the bulk could be beaten or worked into an oblong slab. These slabs were then cut into smaller pieces and placed onto frames to air-dry the tiles before they were fired in the kiln. These early kilns were usually earthern structures with a vent hole in the top to draw air from the fireplace below. The temperature in these kilns reached up to 1000°F (520°C), and the tiles were fired for two days. After the two days, the fire was allowed to go out, but the kiln remained untouched for three days or more, allowing the tiles to cool down slowly. The fired tiles were then removed and prepared for decoration by wiping off any loose sand or dust and lightly moistening the tiles with water.

The original glazes were prepared by first making a glass mass fused with a colored metal oxide. This glass mass was then broken and crushed into a fine powder that was mixed with water. Normally, two glaze coats of white tin oxide were applied to the tile first to conceal the color of the clay. These coats dried quickly, and then a glaze coat was "pounced" onto the tile. In this method, a pattern was outlined on a piece of paper the same size as the tile. This pattern was pricked with a needle to form a stencil, then pumice powder or charcoal was forced through the needle holes to create an outline of the pattern on the coated tile. The pounced pattern was then outlined with a fine brush dipped into glazes made with metal oxide colors. These painted tiles were then placed in the kilns and fired a second time, which effectively fused the colors together to make the decorated tile. For fine polychromatic work, the tile was often fired a third time after having been painted with fragile colors, such as gold or red, that could not take temperatures in excess of 800°F (445°C).

The Egyptians built stone temples, and so they primarily used colored glass glazes to decorate bisque beads and metals. The Mesopotamians used fired glazes as a water seal on their sun-dried brick walls and vaulted ceilings. Mosaic and tiles with incised patterns evolved into fully decorative tiles in bas-relief with handpainted polychromatic details. The art and craft of ceramics, wall tile, and glazed bricks developed into an artful way to protect the palaces and temples from deterioration.

When the Greeks conquered Persia, the chroniclers of

Alexander the Great wrote about the splendor of the bas-relief and beautifully colored tiles that they found in Babylon and Persepolis. Hand-decorated wall tiles and early encaustic tiles lined the important areas of public rooms and spaces of the palaces.

Eventually, the Romans copied the Greek styles of art and architecture, along with their techniques of crafts-manship. The Romans were particularly influenced by the Sumerian tiled and mosaic vaulted ceilings and arches. When the Roman Empire collapsed, this art all but became lost to the Western world, and several centuries passed before glazed tiles were reintroduced to the West from China through Arabia and Turkey.

When the Castillians of northern Spain conquered the

Imagine the delight of the occupants of the New York apartment building that features this lobby (previous page) when they had the walls cleaned and discovered such marvelous tilework! Rambusch Inc. of New York completed this detailed and challenging restoration.

Terra cotta tile flooring was introduced in England by the Dutch and in the American Colonies by the Spanish. It has remained a popular choice for flooring in historic as well as contemporary homes (far left).

The art of handcrafted tile murals has a long history that extends through the Art Deco period. This craft is being revived today through the restoration of authentic designs and the creation of original ones made with time-tested techniques. The tile of this concierge's doorway in Paris has been restored to its original grandeur (left).

*I*n *this unique kitchen, tiles were used almost everywhere. This design scheme could easily be overwhelming, but it works here because of the simple black and white motif and the choice of a neutral floor tile, gray cabinets, and steel ceiling treatment. This is an inspiring example of finely crafted tiles featured in a contemporary room.*

Andalusian Plains in southern Spain, they took possession of the richly ornamented palaces. These buildings were of such luxury and refinement that even the Venetians journeyed to the Alhambra and Seville to wonder at their incredible craftsmanship. Here, walls, floors, window surrounds, wainscoting and pools were lined with glazed tiles painted with complex geometrics, diapers, and foliations. Tiles in bas-relief and with incised designs in blue, green, yellow, black, white, and brown-red were used for archways, counter tops and flooring.

Originally, it was probably the Spanish, inspired by the Moors, who used tiles in the cooking areas. Tiles lined braziers, which, over time, evolved into tile-covered stoves and counter tops. The Dutch adapted the tiled arched projection over the cooking area that originated in Spain. The Dutch were among the first since the Roman Empire to recognize the value of tile to waterseal their walls and floors.

The Dutch began making earthenware tiles in the fourteenth century. Their early tiles were made of red clay, sometimes decorated with lead glazes in tones of yellow, green, black, and brown. One technique refined by the Dutch included the use of a white clay slip fired over the top of the red clay body. This slip sometimes had indentations from a pressed design. The indented design was then filled with colored clay, making an encaustic tile. Another technique used by the Dutch was to apply colored glazes either to the indentations or to the flat white slip to decorate the tile.

By the fifteenth century, the Dutch tiles were ornamented with French Gothic designs and motifs, and they were being exported into Europe through England. However, because these tiles could not withstand the great amount of traffic of the medieval floor, the Dutch floor tile industry did not last long. Instead, polychromatic tiles were used on the walls. These tiles features arabesques and interlaced designs in yellow, blue, white, black, and green.

By the seventeenth century, Holland had become the Western center for tile making. Dutch tiles were used to line cellars, dairies, kitchens, and for the skirting at the base of plaster or wood walls, and for the facing on their large fireplaces and overmantles. Influenced by the Dutch shipping industry, the tile makers painted their tiles with ships, items that the ships imported, vases, animals, birds, as well as religious scenes and Dutch peasants.

In the meantime, Portuguese tile makers expanded tile ornamentation to include large-scale picture tiles and tilework frames that included court scenes, botanical studies, and religious themes. These tiles often covered interior facade walls and walls of garden courtyards.

In the 1600s, European craftsmen began to refine their clay. A clay washing method was used to remove coarse sand, shell fragments, and other impurities. First, the raw materials were mixed with water. Then this mixture was drained through a sieve to remove the excess water, and the clay was kneaded to increase its elasticity. A measure of lime was added to prevent cracking of the clay during the drying process.

The use of ceramic tiles to create heating stoves

Deeply colored glazed tiles have remained a preferred architectural material for fine bathrooms throughout the nineteenth and twentieth centuries. This black tile tub in a contemporary design is complemented by the period mirror hanging above.

brought the tile craftsmen to new levels of creativity during the Baroque and Rococco periods. The ceramic artist was now developing freestanding and interlocking tiles with bas-relief and polychromatic glazes of every hue. Tiles were also handpainted with scenes and other decorations and used as inserts in wood paneling and in fireplace surrounds.

Tile in the New World was heavily influenced by the English designs that had originated in Spain and Holland. As the North American continent developed, the English influence was even more pronounced, except in the Southwest, where tiles were more strongly affected by Spanish and Mexican designs.

Eventually, the use of decorated tile for wall ornamentation in the ancient city of Persepolis was revived when

the beautiful craftsmanship of the East provided the inspiration for designers and craftspeople of the Victorian era. The designers of England's Arts and Crafts movement further elevated tile craftsmanship with their exotic and colorful design and pattern compositions that provided an integration of styles unique for the time. Then, with the revival of the Baroque style in the 1900s, terra cotta tiles became a favorite architectural form during the Art Nouveau and Art Deco periods of the early twentieth century.

The demand today by collectors and museums for the old Delft tiles of Holland and the antique tiles from China, Damascus, Persia, and Turkey are testaments to the continued value and superb quality of this craft. Luckily, countries such as France, Italy, Spain, Portugal, Mexico, and China have revived their handcrafted tile-making craft.

*H*andcrafted
tiles have been embossed and inlaid
with designs for many centuries. Today,
this craft is almost forgotten, and only
provided by a very few craftspeople,
such as L'Esperance, who created all
the tiles on these two pages.

*B*as-relief
and polychromatic glazed tiles have
adorned important residences since
the time of Alexander the Great.
L'Esperance Tile Works revives encaustic
tiles for a contemporary home.

Courtesy L'Esperance Tile Works

Courtesy L'Esperance Tile Works

LINDA ELLETT-SHORE

Linda Ellett-Shore's interest in handcrafted tiles evolved from her talent for sculpting and ceramics. After receiving a degree in ceramic art, she apprenticed at the Moravian Pottery and Tile Works in Doylestown, Pennsylvania. She decided to turn her combination of skills into a practical business, so she founded L'Esperance Tile Works in Albany, New York.

Dedicated to preserving the art of handpressed ceramic tile, Ellett-Shore continues to use production methods employed by pre-industrial craftsmen. The terra-cotta clay she uses is dug locally near the banks of the Hudson River. She often uses plaster molds, such as those originating at the turn of the century, and the decoration of tiles that is being restored is faithfully reproduced by hand. Some modern technology, such as electric kilns, augments the hand design and decoration process to provide custom tiles from all periods for use in contemporary, as well as historic, homes and buildings.

Ellett-Shore continues to study historical tiles. She received a grant to study medieval and Victorian tile-making in England. She visited many authentic working museums as well as countless abbeys and other historic sites. She also located, photographed, and catalogued medieval tiles for her extensive color slide collection that she frequently refers to.

Today, Ellett-Shore's company continues to offer services that include identification and research of tiles, conservation, restoration, and reproduction. L'Esperance also carries many tile designs in stock that are based on turn-of-the century American and English styles. Ellett-Shore's designs, which include encaustic and Delft tiles, are used for walls, hearths, fireplaces, and splashboards.

L'Esperance tiles are found in many historic projects today, including the Lieutenant Governor's Office in the New York State Capitol, Coeymans Historic Stone House in Coeymans, New York, and the Kol Israel Temple in Brooklyn, New York.

*H*and-pressed or embossed tiles are made with a sculpted mold (above). This technique was popular during the Renaissance, and has been revived by Linda Ellett-Shore at L'Esperance, shown here with her husband John Shore (top).

These
lovely and unique tiles were designed
by Sharon Risedorph of Designs in Tile.
Though hand-painted tiles are
expensive, they can be used sparingly
as stunning accents.

Restoration Guidelines

Today, the tile craftsperson is spared the tedious task of preparing the clay, since this is now done by machinery. Furthermore, manufactured clay is strengthened with additives and pressed into a controlled thickness. Sophisticated steel tooling forms the clay into various shapes. The tile industry has been further modernized by power spray equipment and automatically applied decorations that replicate the handpainted look of yesterday.

In spite of this modern technology, there are still many artisans and craftspeople who are designing and hand decorating tiles. There is even a handful of craftspeople who form and fire their tiles by hand before they apply the decorations. The tiles that are the result of this handcrafted work are distinctively rich, in a way that machinery can not reproduce.

The installation of ceramic tile requires special knowledge, skills, and equipment, though the homeowner can do it. In days gone by, tile was always set in a bed of mortar. Today, it is frequently installed with synthetic adhesives that hold the tile in place as well as, if not better than, mortar and grouts. Plastic spacers which come in different sizes proportionate to the size of the tile, can be placed at the corners of the tiles to guide the tile setter to regulate the distance between each tile. Prepare the surface according to manufacturer's instructions and set the tile in place with the help of spacers and adhesive. Then mix the grout and fill the spaces between the tiles. More complicated projects that require cutting the tiles for custom-fitting at the corners and edges can be difficult for the do-it-yourselfer, however. Inexpensive tools do not generally work satisfactorily and some skill must be developed to make a clean edge. If your project requires cutting tiles, it might be best to hire a craftsperson for the job.

Working with a tile craftsperson can be simplified if you do a little research. Visit your local library to look through the available books on ornamental tiles. Photocopy any pictures of illustrated tile patterns that appeal to you, and give these to the craftsperson. Or, tear pages from interior design magazines that illustrate the types of design and colors that you especially like. Using these examples, the artisan can then provide a thumbnail sketch for you and make recommendations for your pro-

ject design. Some craftspeople charge extra for changes you make once work is in progress, so it is important to be very clear about your expectations in the beginning. Finally, you should know that tiny sketches can look good until they are blown up to full scale, when the spaces between the design can become bigger, resulting in an unbalanced look. Because of this you should try to make arrangements to have approval on all final sketches executed to scale, or, at the very least, no smaller than one-half or one-quarter scale.

Part of the uniqueness of handpainted tiles is the variation of color tones on the tiles. The irregular lines and edges that sometimes result from freehand work also add to the character and individuality of the tiles. Although mass-produced manufactured tiles can often do the job for any particular project, the "one-of-a-kind" aspect of handpainted tiles is lost. Some tile factories do employ artisans to create the original pattern, which is then repeated mechanically. Nevertheless, it is really not the same as having each tile handcrafted, and if it is important for you to have the original aspect of each tile that can only come from a craftsperson, the effort of coordinating your ideas with a ceramic artisan will be well worth the time and effort.

Although budgeting for handpainted tiles can be difficult, it is not impossible. One shortcut is to design your project so that it has a random placement of a handpainted tile within a field of plain tiles. A panel inset with handpainted tiles can also be used with factory-manufactured plain tiles, or a special pattern selected for tiles to be used as a border.

The maintenance of any tile surface is very important. The aging process of authentic tiles is hastened by unknowing neglect, and these tiles are expensive to replace. The glazes, though very tough and resilient to moisture, are not indestructible. Grout is especially susceptible to a loss of the water sealing benefits, and its deterioration is aggravated by the use of the wrong cleaning materials. Abrasive scrubbing compounds, bleach, and ammonia all affect the grout surface adversely. If the grout between the tiles is not maintained, moisture will seep down and onto the edges of the tile. This may permit a slight swelling of the tile beneath the glaze, and a

© Maria Pape

deterioration process can begin that can loosen the fired glaze. In addition, the absorption of moisture will result in crazing or cracking of the tile glaze. This will lead to the growth of mildew and bacteria, which will result in telltale stains and discoloring just under the glaze surface. Additionally, crazing, left untreated, results in the absorption of dirt into the cracks. Tile floors and walls around bathtubs and sinks should be cleaned periodically and

resealed to maintain the water sealing benefits. The special supplies for this job can be purchased at a retail or wholesale shop that caters to the tile and marble trades.

Handcrafted tiles are versatile and can work a special magic from the bathroom to the kitchen and in any other room. The colors have a depth and richness that surpass that of flat-painted surfaces and have earned tile a very special place in both history and our homes.

A

classic hand-painted Japanese screen introduces the 'international' aspect of this design scheme. The staircase follows provincial lines; the overdoor is English "spiderweb"; the wainscot is hand-painted faux stone; the floor tiles are Spanish.

BRICK

Brick makers and masons have been helping to build structures for the people of the civilized world since before written history, and every major culture has contributed to the development of the art and science of brick making and masonry. The peoples of many lands and almost every culture have been quick to establish brick making practices using the materials that were available locally. No matter what type of clay they were made from, universally, and through time, the bricks were reinforced with grass or straw fibers. However, the climate and natural resources of specific areas caused the brick makers to develop methodologies that differed in subtle ways. For instance, in the southern zones of North America, where alluvial clay (also known as adobe) and hot sunshine are abundant, earlier builders frequently depended on sun-dried adobe bricks as an inexpensive building material. In the colder, damp climates of the north, brick makers had to rely on kilns to harden their clay.

Courtesy The Bulmer Brick & Tile Co., Ltd

Brickwork
is not always arranged horizontally or
vertically, but can be arranged in
interesting patterns, as in these cusped
arches and windows. Bricks for the
restoration of this English church were
hand made by Bulmer Brick &
Tile Company, Ltd.

Though
the look of this room is rustic, the
authentic brickwork is so beautiful that
it brings warmth to the style
(previous page).

An example of the beauty of brickwork was discovered when Alexander the Great drove Darius III from the city of Persepolis in ancient Persia. Alexander and his soldiers were stunned by the opulence of this ancient Middle Eastern capital. Great walls of sun dried brick in bas-relief with stylized lions and parading nobility, as well as other symbols of power and wealth, lined the squares and stairs to the royal palace. The entrance facade was faced with bas-relief brick decorated with fired polychromatic glazes. The glory of the master brick makers and masons of ancient Persia was evident in the ceiling of the throne room in the palace, which was completely covered with silver. Such cosmopolitan richness and beauty had never before been seen by the Greeks, whose toughness was fostered in the austerity of their impoverished homeland. It is claimed that the treasury of one city of the Middle Eastern empire was ten times as great as the full national treasury of Alexander's homeland.

Nonetheless, the militant Greeks preferred the solid security and protective strength of stone and marble. Also, although the ancient Egyptians were avid brick makers, and had even enslaved entire villages for the mixing, forming, and drying of brick, it was the Roman Empire that passed the joy and beauty of ornamental brick work along to the Western world. The peoples of the Western world then passed the brick making methodology to each successive generation for centuries to come, causing brick making to become a popular craft throughout Europe. Eventually the craft moved to England from Spain, where the Moors had maintained the techniques, as well as from Rennaissance Italy, where craftsmen were busily reviving the ancient craft of sgraffito (incised stucco). These stone and stucco craftsmen from the eastern regions of the Roman Empire painstakingly incised, by hand, artistic patterns into the stone or stucco buildings. Their work served as the creative force that brickmakers emulated for years to come in the craft of pressed brick.

To create this pressed, patterned brick, the brick maker originally used a tool to carve a pattern into the brick while the clay mixture was still damp. The pattern dried into the brick as a permanent decorative part of it. Soon, another method evolved that would make the decorative process even simpler. The desired pattern was carved into a stamp, generally made of wood or clay. This stamp was pressed into the brick mixture, thus eliminating the hand carving process, and saving untold hours of time. The pattern was determined in advance, and the design in each brick was scaled to contribute to the overall decorative effect as the bricks were laid to build the structure.

This pressing technique was further developed in Europe in the late 1800s with the invention of the steam-driven brick-pressing machine. Mounted with brass and iron molds, these machines were able to stamp out brick with every conceivable design, including French, English, and German Gothic patterns, as well as Georgian, Norman, Italian classical, Oriental floral, and American colonial patterns. Many of these designs were introduced on 5″ x 10″ x 2½″ (12.8 cm x 25.6 cm x 6.4 cm) and 10″ x 10″ x 2½″ (25.6 cm x 25.6 cm x 6.4 cm) bricks, which had their roots in the ancient frieze walls of Rome and earlier Persia.

At about this time, the expansion of the British empire, and the growing wealth of the English middle class led the brick makers of England to develop their techniques to include the making of ornamental brick, in the manner of the ancient Romans. These Victorian brick makers produced hundreds of patterns of conventionalized decorative brick, specially designed for use in totally integrated design concepts. These pressed patterns provided the brick mason with the opportunity to create beautifully patterned walls, walks, and fireplaces.

The English consumer was now able to select decorative brick from illustrated lithograph catalogues that displayed a variety of architectural decorations. These brick catalogues contained many specialty bricks of different sizes and textures, pressed with floral motifs, vines, leaves, birds, diamonds, pyramids, and other shapes. Ultimately, the Victorian middle class, like the citizens of Rome, were able to draw upon the rich vocabulary of design from the far reaches of the world. The exuberance and expertise of the craftsmen of that era are still apparent in the brick work that lines the streets of many cities in England, Canada, and the United States.

In fact, it could be said that rows of brick houses in Britain, Canada, and America owe their existence to the Great Fire of London in 1666. It caused such devastation that the Rebuilding Act of 1667 was put into effect, which dictated the use of brick and stone for reconstruction of houses. The results can still be seen today in the beautiful Queen Anne and Georgian houses that are decorated with ornamental brick patterns and dormers, corbels, gables, and doorways finished in the Classic Revivalism style. The period following the fire also saw half-timber Tudor structures with filled brick spaces in the traditional basket weave, herringbone, and other rustic patterns combined with various sizes of brick and masonry, which together formed the structures.

Brick continued to be popular throughout the industrialized Victorian period, and it was an important building material during the boom that found neighborhood tenement housing crowding the factory towns that had sprung up across England. At the same time, though decorative brick did not come into wide use in America until the late 1700's, and it wasn't until the early 1800's that decorative brick was made on the North American continent, brick was being used in the colonies as the primary building material for homes and commercial buildings.

While the Industrial Age revolutionized brick making with the steam-powered pressing machines, it also eventually brought about the demise of the flourishing market for decorative brick, along with the craft and individual skill of the brick mason. The mason had created walls of artistic expression through the placement and variation in texture of the bricks resulting in vertical, horizontal or diagonal patterns that serve to complement the other projections and architectural details of the building. With machine made bricks, such skillful creation was not so rewarding.

Toward the end of the Victorian period, glazed terra cotta (clay bisque building blocks with fire-glazed coatings) and color glazed brick were introduced at the Paris Expo at the turn of the century. These exciting materials were soon incorporated in the revival of French Classic and new Edwardian "Grand Manner" architecture.

With the turn of the twentieth century and the continued growth of the "freestyle" Arts and Crafts movement in architecture (which had its roots in England), the brick makers began to move away from ornamental-patterned brick in order to supply an increasing demand for more "natural" products. The brick industry concentrated on the mass production of plain bricks, textured bricks, or bricks in different colored clays, such as buff, tan, light gray, and red. Glazed bricks became increasingly popular, as did decorative tiles, and brick makers and masons remained in demand until the 1940s, when decorative bricks (with pressed designs) stopped being made. The attendant craft of the mason, who designed and laid elaborate arches, window trims, and other architectural patterns, also declined until masonry was performed by only a select few. The herringbone brick patterns and other basket-weave designs, were temporarily lost to modern man, as were the patterned arches made of tapered, rubbed, or cut brick, and other designs that had been so common during the Georgian and early Victorian periods.

The economic decline experienced by most nations after World War I also forced a change in home-building styles. Architectural designs became less ornamental and

© Maria Pape

creative, as advancing economic pressures caused the sacrifice of the fanciful cornice embellishments, stacked projections, and trim patterns as well as whimsical foliations, florals, and other design references to nature.

Technology ushered in factories, with machinery and assembly lines that produced bricks to standard sizes, without variation or decoration. The art of decorative brick making began to disappear as a more serious society demanded flat, austere brick surfaces. The "modernists" and rising cost considerations in construction came together to help bring about the new "international style" of modern architecture.

The precision of fine masonry work is apparent in the floor and walls of this contemporary wine cellar

Brick Fireplaces

Of all the practices that fell into the mason's realm, the fireplace alone represents hospitality, and, as such, it has been viewed through the ages as the true center of the home and the mason's art. Styles of fireplaces, mantels, and hearths have always varied greatly from culture to culture and period to period. However, the desire for a beautiful fixture that also functions properly has continued to be of major importance as civilization developed through the ages. Even the great artist Raphael was once commissioned to design a smokeless fireplace—thus combining beauty and function.

The Romans may have been the first to develop a moderately efficient method of central heating. They constructed vents in the floors of their rooms that led to an area below where slaves maintained fires and made steam that rose to heat the upper rooms. However, with the collapse of the Roman Empire and the wars that followed, this technology of heating was lost. Medieval Europeans suffered in their great, drafty, stone manor houses.

Records from the Dark Ages clearly show the arrangement of private homes and castles in this period of history, and the fireplace played a critical part in the design scheme. The lord's estate was generally arranged so that the main hall contained a huge fireplace, around which all events took place. A large table was constructed so that the lord of the manor could sit with his back to the fire when he dined. The British craftsmen of that period went a step further, and constructed a long bench with only a support rail, not a solid back, so the heat from the fire was not blocked. This rail could be swung from back to front so that one could sit either facing the fire or with one's back to the fire, allowing a choice of seating and the necessary warmth.

The height of the ceiling in these rooms had much to do with the efficiency of the fireplace in heating the room. Unlike the English, who kept their ceilings comparatively low and more in scale with domestic comfort, the French court became obsessed with architectural styles

that were designed primarily for their display of wealth and power. Because of this, their palaces were extremely drafty, with the fireplaces' heating ability significantly diminished. The great Palace of Versailles was so drafty that the king placed an upholstered sedan chair before the fireplace in an attempt to protect himself from the creeping cold of the great marble halls. The bed chamber of the mistress of Versailles was eventually modified to include an inner chamber of draped walls, and a bed that was also draped. Although some disdainfully felt that this three-layered bedroom was an example of flamboyant luxury, in reality it was designed to inhibit the sweeping drafts so that the mistress could sleep as comfortably and warmly as possible. This decorative scheme was adapted by the masses, and often the warmest place in many houses was the bed, behind the draperies and canopies.

The Italian Renaissance influenced a revival of craftsmanship in the eighteenth century that resulted in some significant advances in technology and design. Design elegance along with functional perfection were maximized in England in the 1700s. In 1748, the excavations of Herculaneum and Pompeii were begun by the French, and continued for another 100 years. In 1754, Englishman Robert Adams visited the excavations in Italy and took back home with him accurate measurements and sketches of the architectural findings he observed there. In 1762, he was assigned the position of Architect to King George III, and his business partner and brother, James Adams, succeeded him in this position in 1768. One other brother, John, was also active in the family business, but it was Robert who achieved the greatest fame for his interior design compositions and the designs of some of the finest homes in England. In fact, during the colonial years of America and Canada, most of the craftsmen in the colonies had still been trained in Europe. Many of them were familiar with the *Golden Section* of a two to three ratio in building fireplaces, which was revived by the Adams brothers, from the ancient Greeks and incorporated into their designs. In America, almost all colonial fireplaces were based on this proportional design scheme, which dictates that the height of a fireplace is two times, and the width three times a given measurement.

During this period in America and Canada, fireplaces enjoyed a temporary return to their original massive scale, sometimes covering as much as half a wall. They served as a cook stove and an oven for baking bread, as well as the primary source of heat for the area.

The craftsmen who had migrated to the New World colonies and specialized in designing and constructing fireplaces, usually built them in local materials, using rock or brick from nearby kilns. Occasionally, they would use a combination of brick and stone for the design, and the flue of the fireplace was sometimes made from metal. The design of the chimney was critical, since a chimney that drew correctly was essential. A beautifully designed fireplace that didn't properly heat a room or that belched smoke into the house sometimes actually drove the inhabitants from the house. Historians have recorded incidents when huge European manor houses were abandoned because the fireplace flues could not be made to work properly. Without heat, the house was virtually unlivable.

Eventually, industrialization, combined with the decline in the number of masons who could construct a fireplace that worked properly, led the Victorians to rely on the new, improved heating inventions, such as portable stoves and coal burner boxes. In America, Ben Franklin invented a slow-burning grate that was modified, perfected, and used extensively in the nineteenth century for heating homes. The fireplace diminished in size and, in fact, began to be built with incorrect proportions, affecting both the beauty and the usefulness of a fixture that had been so important throughout the ages.

The nature of your brick project will help you determine the type of craftspeople you will need. Some masons, for example, are exceptionally experienced with fireplaces, others with patterned brick walls or curved arches. A call to the local masons guild can be helpful in locating a mason with the expertise in the area required for your project. Most masons do not do cleanings, and your best bet is to contact your local conservator or preservationist for referrals here. Query carefully about areas of expertise, and your project will be better for it.

Generally a brick mason will be able to complete your installation as well as provide the materials necessary. Occasionally, the mason will have to work with a brick maker, particularly if the bricks being replaced or patched are especially old and unique. There are also several companies that make bricks in custom sizes and shapes. These specialty companies can often adequately replicate the authentic oversized corner bricks, pediment bricks, and arch bricks, as well as stamp the decorative patterns of some of the simpler antique ornamental bricks.

Today, the functional fireplace has all but completely lost its significance as the major source of heat and as a cook stove. However, just as it was in the days of the great hall of the English lords, the fireplace has retained its symbolic role as the center of domestic harmony. The fireplace today stands as a beautiful and romantic focal point in design, and a wonderful medium of artistic expression for the brick maker and the mason.

*H*andcrafted

decorative bricks are almost obsolete. However, craftsman Peter Minter and his artisans have continued this nearly lost art at his Bulmer Brick & Tile Company in England. Decorated bricks are made with handcrafted methods and natural materials (right). Some of Minter's faithfully reproduced, hand-molded bricks are shown above.

Restoration Guidelines

Today, fireplaces are prefabricated in factories and are guaranteed to draw correctly. This prefabricated unit is set into place (including the flue), and the brick mason has only to lay the bricks that surround the works on the inside. On the outside, he lays bricks around the flue, and this then becomes the chimney. Although today's fireplaces have lost much of the artistic flavor of the fireplaces of old, they have gained enormously from the technology that exists, making a working fireplace something that is very much taken for granted.

Nevertheless, even today, assessing brick damage and brick replacement needs—particularly where older authentic brickwork is concerned—is always best left to an expert well versed in preservation. One reason for this is that brick, whether it makes up a fireplace or a wall, is composed with a thin protective outer layer that should never be penetrated. Once this protective layer is broken, the brick will begin to deteriorate rapidly, making extensive replacement necessary.

With this in mind, brick should never be cleaned by a nonprofessional, except possibly for a light cleaning with soap and water and a natural bristle brush. Experts should be brought in to perform any other cleaning or

restoration techniques that might be required.

Damage also needs to be handled by an expert. Simple precautions, however, can often prevent damage in the first place. In the fireplace, for example, brick can be affected by the very fire it contains. A too hot fire can "burn out" the fireplace. In other words, because brick is merely a fired clay, excessive heat can weaken it to the point where the brick will begin the conversion process back to its basic elements. Similarly, the mortar that holds the bricks together may deteriorate when exposed to very high temperatures. Because of this, the mortar should be checked periodically, and the bricks repointed if necessary. Also, there is often a high rate of deterioration in the chimney stack at the top where the heat concentrates. One of the most important jobs a chimney sweep performs is removing the carbon deposits from the lining of the chimney, which, if left to accumulate, tend to increase the heat buildup on the brick itself.

Often the need for brick repair or replacement occurs when it is discovered that a few original bricks are missing from around the fireplace or at a window or door. Historic houses built with handmade bricks or bricks that are of an unusual shape, size, or clay may require concentrated attention to detail in order to make the closest possible match. Matching the original brick can be very difficult, since aging and environmental factors sometimes alter the texture and color of the brick. Consequently, it is sometimes a good idea to locate an area of the house where you can remove a few bricks to replace damaged ones in a more visible area. You can purchase newer bricks (or even older ones that don't quite match) and install them where you removed the original bricks. By doing this, you will be able to retain the visual integrity of the wall or structure where it would be obvious, and at the same time, hide your repair work in a less visible area. Another solution is to remove a few bricks from the damaged area. Take these to used brick yards or building wrecking yards and use them to select bricks that match as closely as possible with the bricks needing repair or replacement.

You will want to take care when buying mortar as well. Colored mortars are available that may more closely match the original mortar on your house. This is important because if the brick mason uses an unblended white mortar, you will be able to see the repaired areas, regardless of how closely your replacement bricks match. Check with your local brick suppliers, since many of them also carry the tinted mortars and cleaning materials for bricks and pavers. Mortars may also be custom-tinted. After inquiring which brick suppliers in your area do this, give them a sample of the original mortar. They will match it, then supply you with preformulated bags of mortar mix.

Cutting costs for quality brick repair or replacement is not easy. There are only a few brick masons who are adequately trained for this authentic craft. You can reduce some of your costs, however, with careful advanced planning. Decide which one will be the best for your project. Schedule your project so that it can be done properly, with enough time given to insure an authentic look. The craftsperson can advise you on how much of which supplies you should purchase for the job. However, do the research, selection, and ordering of the materials yourself, instead of paying the craftsperson to do this work. You'll also have more control over the selection of material and the overall cost. Once you have determined the best possible supplies, order them far enough in advance so that you have them on site when the craftspeople arrive to do the work. Make certain you've received exactly what you ordered and not too little material. A budget can be exceeded very quickly if you must pay a craftsperson to wait either for materials to arrive at the beginning of a project, or for additional materials to be delivered after they run out in the middle.

The nature of your brick project will help you determine the type of craftsmen you will need. Some masons, for example, are exceptionally experienced with fireplaces, others with patterned brick walls or curved arches. A call to the local masons guild can be helpful in locating a mason with the expertise in the area required for your project. Most masons do not do cleanings, and your best bet is to contact your local conservator or preservationist for referrals here. Query carefully about areas of expertise, and your project will be better for it.

Generally a brick mason will be able to complete your installation as well as provide the materials necessary. Occasionally, the mason will have to work with a brick maker, particularly if the bricks being replaced or patched are especially old and unique. There are also several companies that make bricks in custom sizes and shapes. These speciality companies can often adequately replicate the authentic oversized corner bricks, pediment bricks, and arch bricks, as well as stamp the decorative patterns of some of the simpler antique ornamental bricks.

Today, the functional fireplace has all but completely lost its significance as the major source of heat and as a cooker. However, just as it was in the days of the great hall of the English lords, the fireplace has retained its symbolic role as the center of domestic harmony. The fireplace today stands as a beautiful and romantic focal point in design, and a wonderful medium of artistic expression for the brick maker and the mason.

The brick fireplace and hand-glazed tile flooring complement classic Georgian wood windows and wicker furnishings with elegance and practicality in a contemporary room.

Craftsman

Tom Bird from Bulmer Brick & Tile stokes the kiln (below). Bulmer Brick & Tile is one of a dwindling number of companies who specialize in brick restoration and replication, including hand-molding and cutting. Peter Minter, owner of the company, stands in front of the kiln (right).

Bulmer

supplied bricks for the restoration of Compton Wynyates in Warwickshire, replicating bricks from the sixteenth century (below right).

PETER MINTER and TOM MCGRATH

British craftsman Peter Minter is the owner of the Bulmer Brick & Tile Co., which was originally purchased by his father fifty years ago. Located in Bulmer Nr. Sudbury, Suffolk, England, this family business has provided Peter Minter with a childhood and adult life that has revolved around the age-old craft of making bricks by hand.

Bulmer bricks are made from London bed clay, which has been dug almost continuously since early Tudor times. This clay, when fired, produces the traditional mellow red bricks associated with many of the outstanding historical buildings throughout England. All of Minter's molds are handmade, and from these molds he handcrafts the bricks identically to those originally found in nearly any period of historical architecture. Although Minter has an impressive array of existing molds, he is also frequently called upon to produce custom molds for specific historic projects. Molds for these jobs are produced to exactly match the requirements of each building.

Handmade Bulmer bricks are found in a staggering number of historical structures, including such impressive edifices as Hampton Court, Windsor Castle, the Tower of London, Old Hall, Lincoln's Inn, Oxburgh Hall, Compton Wynyates, Great Fosters, and Layer Marney Towers, among others.

Architectural students often visit Minter to observe his brick making techniques firsthand. One such student was American Tom McGrath, who also traveled to Italy to study early Roman brick making techniques. Later, he studied at the Vatican, where he learned about historic terra cotta and tile manufacture as well. Eventually, he was awarded a grant from the American National Endowment for the Arts to study in England, which allowed his period of study with Peter Minter.

Now owner of his own firm, High Brooms, Inc., in Boston, Mass., McGrath does terra cotta tile restoration, writes specifications for masonry work, and, when called upon, travels around the country to custom make special orders for companies that do not otherwise provide the service.

Courtesy The Bulmer Brick & Tile Co., Ltd.

This is the kiln that has been used to fire Bulmer bricks since 1937 (left). It takes three weeks for the firing process: a week to load; a week to fire; and a week to unload. Here are three chimneys in the process of authentic restoration by Bulmer (below left).

Wooden molds such as these are used to shape hand-pressed bricks (below).

Courtesy The Bulmer Brick & Tile Co., Ltd.

Courtesy The Bulmer Brick & Tile Co., Ltd.

WOOD

Almost all ancient tribal groups developed construction techniques of post-and-beam, with the type of wood used determined by the species of trees that grew in the local area. But early on, man also recognized the beauty and versatility of wood as a building and decorative material.

Wood carving has been a favored pastime for man from before recorded history. The gold-clad, color-inlaid, carved sarcophagi and chairs from the tombs of the Egyptian pharaoahs are some of the better known examples of this craft. The ancient Egyptians were exceptional carvers in many mediums. They developed the technique of using carved wooden forms as the structural base for plaster bas-relief walls.

After the collapse of the Roman Empire, the Vandals (or Goths) swept through Europe, burning and pillaging villages and towns. Security became a top priority for people everywhere. Wood gave way to stone as the predomi-

*M*agnificently *carved doorways are a visitor's introduction to the personality and tastes of the owners of a home. These elaborately carved doors are the point of entry into a Mexican puebla (above and right). Their beauty is evident despite the need for restoration.*

*T*his *beautifully hand-polished wood paneled room has been meticulously restored. The fireplace has been accentuated in the Georgian manner and is highlighted by a painting in a gilded frame.*

*T*he *versatility of handcrafted wood is apparent in this room (previous page), where it has been used for moldings, columns, window casings, spindles, pilasters, surrounds, and the fireplace mantle.*

nant construction material because it is less flammable. The stone construction techniques left behind by the Romans were adapted by the British and other European groups into a style now known as Gothic.

Most Gothic design is an adaptation of natural forms, and the Gothic arch and column is believed to have been inspired by the great forests of northern Europe. These forests had large ancient trees that grew so tall that the upper arches created an arched canopy.

It was during this period that craftsmen of different ethnic groups developed their own national preferences, incorporating favorite flora and animal motifs into the Gothic style, creating what was to become the first Western international style. Carvings with natural forms were combined with mythological beings, in the manner of the Byzantine art styles of the times.

In England, wood carvers simply adapted the designs and patterns of the Celtic wicker workers and basket weavers, adorning wood moldings, chairs, panels, banisters, and other carvings with woven motifs. There is evidence that the first crosses made in England during the conversion to Christianity were constructed of interlaced wicker, and that the wooden and stone crosses of later times were carved to replicate those early ones.

Knights and warriors returning home from the Crusades brought stories of the riches of Eastern cities and cultures. Separate quarters for women and resting rooms stirred the Western imagination. Bedrooms and sitting rooms were built, and the carved banister and stairs that the Crusaders had witnessed in Eastern harems were adapted to English tastes. These designs were soon in every major dwelling, symbols of international sophistication, learning, and wealth. By the Elizabethan period, bannisters were massive with complex designs and elegantly carved posts.

The conquering Normans introduced wood paneling into early British design. They also brought decorative painted rafters and walls. Gradually, the arts of the wood carver and master carpenter began to replace fabric wall hangings and tapestries in England's castles.

The knowledge of woodworking expanded significantly when peace began to settle upon Europe during the Middle Ages. Wood had long been appreciated not only for its beauty and elegance but also for its acoustical and insulative qualities. Wood converted the damp, cold, echoing halls of the Middle Ages stone structures into the warmer and more livable environments that we value today.

Eventually, wood became such an important material in England that a period piece is most easily identified today by the type of wood it is made from. Oak was used

The lustrous ash paneling in this room is not as expensive as it looks (left). Large sheets of wood were secured to the walls, then the grid panel surrounds were laminated on top. This procedure eliminates the time- and money-consuming techniques required to carefully fit each panel, but preserves the luxurious effect.

The details in architectural wood carvings are often very intricate and reflect the refined skill and craftsmanship required of their creator. In this room, notice the delicate workmanship of the panel surrounds which serve to emphasize the grain pattern of the wood.

from the earliest times through the reigns of Henry VIII and Elizabeth, for example. Both Henry and Elizabeth imported large numbers of Italian craftsmen to England, an estimated 40,000 during the reign of Elizabeth alone. Although Henry wanted craftsmen to copy the more classical palatial styles of Renaissance France, his death put those ideas to rest. Instead, comfort and a visible relationship with nature remained important to the British. Ignoring the Renaissance principles that were being followed elsewhere, the British craftsmen built rooms with lower ceilings for better heating and designed paneling and wainscoting from dyed woods. The major building style ignored classical Italian principles as well, but remained the native Celtic post-and-beam design detailed with Gothic motifs, which came to be referred to as Tudor.

When the Scottish Stuarts took the throne of England, they brought their preference for the French classical revival styles to England. France continued to develop the Baroque arts and crafts that had been refined under Louis

XIII, and the Stuarts managed to introduce these designs under their reign.

The Puritan Revolution, along with the great fire of London, resulted in a building boom in England. The new styles were also influenced by the returning political refugees who had been living on the Continent during the civil wars of the Stuart reign. Although oak continued to be used, softer woods such as pine and ash that were delicately carved also came into vogue. With the end of the Stuart reign and the marriage of English Mary to Dutch William, the age of walnut and of Dutch influence with more gracious curving lines in design, was firmly established in England.

During the reign of Queen Anne, the English love of nature was reinforced further, and the scale of British interiors remained in human proportions, generating warmth and intimacy. Wood remained a favorite material for walls and ceilings, and the English wood carver reached new heights of perfection in his technique. Oak

was too open grained and hard for the relief carving on cornices and moldings that were being used for the ornate door and paneling surrounds. Softer woods, such as walnut, were used instead so that the carvers could create the more intricate undercut motifs. The overdoor ornaments and chimney pieces richly carved with flowers, swags, fruit, foliage, urns, baskets, and half-round figures were cut from basswood, pine, lime, deal, and cedar. Wooden fluted pilasters with heavily carved capitals were crested with cornices and ceiling moldings. Carved door and window surrounds became important design elements, while flooring was most commonly made of plain, well-joined boards.

In the Georgian period, the wood carvings became more intricate, with even deeper undercuts. Door surrounds and pediments remained important, and painted paneling became more common, particularly pine, which was frequently painted with white, gray, greenish gray, or blue-green, and embellished with gilding. Wood inlay, or parquet was used for flooring in more affluent houses. It was not until the 1700s that mahogany replaced walnut as the primary home furnishing wood in England.

During the reign of King George I, the English craftsman Thomas Chippendale, with his father, moved to London. By this time, Rennaissance, Gothic, and Oriental patterns, modified to suit British tastes, were firmly rooted in England. Chippendale's father was a noted English cabinetmaker, and it was this background that enabled Chippendale to formalize the British sense of design and craftsmanship in wood. While Chippendale borrowed many of his designs from the prevailing international styles, he also successfully mixed Flemish, Spanish, French, Chinese, and Gothic features. His reputation was so great that he received many honors during his lifetime, and his styles were copied around the world, particularly in the new American colonies. During this period, Chippendale and the other wood carvers of England set standards for quality, workmanship, and attention to detail and proportions that are still sought today.

Wood was abundant in the New World, and settlers there used it many ways. While Europe as a whole was experiencing an extended period of opulence in interior design, essential materials such as paint and wall coverings were in short supply in the colonies. The colonists had, through necessity, simplified European design to meet their needs. Local woods were used and the scale was modified. Immigrants from Scandinavia built wood structures that led to the log cabin in cold climates. Flemish shipboard lapping was used to clad the houses on the

chilly windswept eastern coast (later known as Cape Cod style). The entrance to Thomas Jefferson's historic Monticello house was made from grooved wood that was sand painted to look like stone.

Both the Canadians and the colonists continued to enjoy ties with France, and were influenced by the French Court arts that had developed craftsmanship with palatial grandeur. Additionally, the French craftsmen from the countryside had developed their own style—French Provincial—which also influenced design styles in Canada and the New World. Nevertheless, after the American Revolution, English styles continued as a major force in both the United States and Canada.

Back in England, the middle class had gained new wealth and position by Queen Victoria's time, and the demand for housing increased substantially. Elaborate and expensive classical styles that had been adapted from the Italian Rennaissance gave way to the revivalism of Gothic styles. The veranda (taken from a bungalow style in Bengal, India) was popularized, and the intricately carved wood ventilators were used to decorate Victorian homes. Gradually, machine-milled wood moldings and gingerbread eliminated the need for costly, time-consuming hand carving.

The Arts and Crafts Movement encouraged a return to handmade appointments, however. Although wood craftsmen joined together with other craftsmen in the decorative arts to develop a new style that evolved into the crafts bungalow style in America, this was short-lived as mass production replaced craftsmanship and fine joinery. Lamentably, the distinctive individuality of the art of the wood craftsman was lost in all of this industrialization.

*T*his hand-carved doorway pediment, adjoining arch molding and symmetrically placed pilasters are typical examples of the English craftsman's adaptation of classic Roman concepts, a style that subsequently became known as Georgian (above top).

*T*his hardwood door features finely crafted carving, joinery, and finishing, as well as specially made metal finger plates (above).

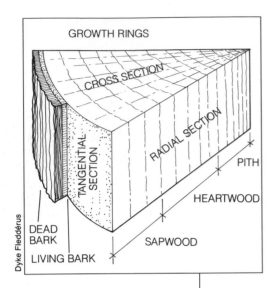

GROWTH RINGS

CROSS SECTION

RADIAL SECTION

TANGENTIAL SECTION

PITH

HEARTWOOD

SAPWOOD

DEAD BARK

LIVING BARK

Dyke Fleddérus

© Maria Pape

Lumber

is graded according to where it comes from in the tree (above). Heartwood, from the middle section of the tree, is the most beautiful and durable. Sapwood is younger, less durable, and usually lighter in color. The nutrients travel through the pith, making this wood soft; it does dry out eventually, but often cracks. When high-grade lumber is milled, the pith and sapwood is usually discarded.

The

grand staircase has been an important element in country estates in Europe. Here, the carefully scaled, tapered wood columns create a sense of modern design that complements the hand-turned wood balustrades and moldings. The wave patterned wood moldings under each step and along the mezzanine provide crowning touches (right).

Wood Growth and Lumbering Techniques

The beauty in the grain and color of wood reflects the history and life span of the tree. The growth of a tree, which occurs only in the spring and summer, is determined by the amount of rainfall each year, and the soil nutrients available. In turn, the growth rate of the trees determines the size of the cells, and variations in cell growth, from year to year and tree to tree, create the grain patterns. The cell itself is thin and grows in an elongated shape from the root stock upwards. An important pattern is created by the cells that flow from the center of the trunk or branch outward toward the bark. These cells are referred to as wood rays and when cut, appear as striae (silver grain, flecking, or tigering).

When wood is cut, its natural grain is exposed in a pattern that is directly related to the cutting method used. When the wood is plain sawn (sliced tangential to the annual layers of the growth rings), the long vertical cell growth is exposed in nested patterns that move toward the ends of the board, with the annual growth ring contours radiating toward the edge of the board. This distinctive pattern is caused by the difference in growth rate between the softer, fast-growing spring wood and the denser, slower-growing summer wood. When wood is quarter-sawn, an additional pattern is created by exposing the grain of the wood rays, or cells, that grow from the center of the plant, called the pith, toward the bark, or

outer layer. The wood rays generally appear lighter and reflect more light than the annual growth rings that result in the vertical grains. Both the summer wood, which appears darker than spring wood, and the wood rays are harder than the other cells of the plant. Because of this, quarter-sawn wood has traditionally been used for flooring and fine furniture since it is stronger and more durable than other cuts of wood.

Wood, when it is first cut, contains large amounts of water and must be dried after cutting. It can take as long as a year to air dry, or "season," wood. As the wood loses water, it shrinks. This shrinkage is not equally distributed, which can cause warping. Eventually, if the stress becomes so extreme that the grain can no longer remain bonded, the wood will split.

While modern technology has decreased the seasoning time of wood through kiln drying, it has also created new problems for the wood craftsperson. Frequently, kiln-dried wood loses moisture at a more rapid rate than is desirable. Because of this, when the raw plank is cut into the thinner planks used by the craftsperson, the damper, inner core will often swell and warp. When wood is air dried, however, the loss of water is slower, and shrinkage will occur more evenly. For this reason, many wood craftspeople prefer to also age the wood after it has first been cut. During earlier periods, many woodworkers allowed their wood to season near where it would be used so that it would fully adapt to that particular climate.

One of the major challenges to the wood craftsperson is shape. Wood-bearing plants exist only in round or oblong shapes, yet the planks, boards, siding, and veneers needed for home furnishings are all flat. Banisters, rails, balustrades, and some moldings, on the other hand, are round, but they still must be honed down to the size and form necessary.

Carving is the skill most often used to achieve the shapes needed. Carving could be described as the removal of material not wanted, and it is an art that is precise and requires substantial talent. The carver begins by removing the large areas first. As the block of wood begins to take shape, the artist uses smaller blades, gouges, and chisels for more delicate cuts. As the work progresses, the tool blades become even smaller, until only filing and sanding is required to remove the unwanted material. The final outcome is controlled by the artist's ability to "see" when and where to stop removing wood. If the chisel gouges too deep, or a piece is accidentally chipped in the wrong place, the piece can be ruined. Only time, talent, and accumulated expertise can result in the skills that are needed to create an architectural work of wood art.

The hand tools used to carve wood have changed little since ancient Egyptian times. Originally, wood was hand-cut, gouged, chiseled, and rasped. Craftsmen scraped wood and rubbed it smooth with grit and polish. Today, the methods for these tasks have been greatly improved. Stronger, tempered metal has been used to improve the quality of the tools as they have also become more specialized. In addition, the Machine Age brought about a revolution in how wood was processed, and today automatic lathes, power drills, and saws eliminate many of the time-consuming steps from yesteryear. The cuts achieved with diamond drill bits are as precise as those made by dentists' tools and provide for a fast and controlled removal of the unwanted pieces of wood. Primary shapes are quickly sliced away from the wood block or plank, eliminating the original hand process that would have taken a single craftsman several days. Planes and routers, mounted with sharp, custom-ground blades and rotated by powerful motors, remove the excess layers of the wood plank to begin the process of shaping squared edges, rounded edges, curvilinear faces, and incised insets (reveals). With all this, however, what has not changed is the amount of loving care a craftsperson must give to each creation.

Courtesy Silverton Victorian Millworks

Courtesy Silverton Victorian Millworks

*S*ilverton
Mills begins the process of creating architectural moldings by planing raw hardwood timber into planks (above).

*L*athing
equipment with special steel blades is used to cut decorative shapes and incised lines into wood planks to create moldings (left).

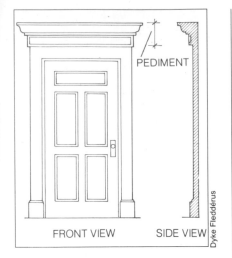

FRONT VIEW   SIDE VIEW

PEDIMENT

Dyke Fleddérus

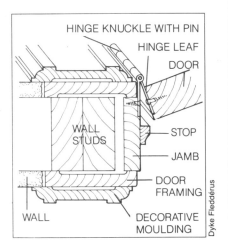

HINGE KNUCKLE WITH PIN

HINGE LEAF

DOOR

STOP

JAMB

DOOR FRAMING

DECORATIVE MOULDING

WALL STUDS

WALL

Dyke Fleddérus

This cut-away view of a door jamb with a mortise hinge set door, illustrates the complicated engineering that goes into hanging a door (above).

Victorian door treatments reflect classic Georgian design (top). Wide sashes replace columns, and the base and the pediment form an unbroken cornice molding.

This Victorian-style oak door has a leaded and beveled glass 'view', reticulated moldings, and symmetrical finials (woodwork by Silverton Mills, right.)

Courtesy Silverton Victorian Millworks

Doors

Historically, the front door has been one of the most important features of the household. As the entry to the home, it provided an eloquent first impression for visitors. It was the wood carver's task to create a statement of status and security for the people who lived behind the door. During the Middle Ages, massive doors repelled invaders and projecting metal pins often served to discourage the less determined. In later periods, the door and doorway continued to indicate affluence and social position.

The Greeks adapted door designs from the eastern part of their empire, including the use of doorknockers and other hardware for ornamentation. It was the Spanish however, who made doors with carved panels put together with tongue and groove joinery and ornamental nails with heads in decorative shapes such as pyramids, stars, flowers, and the like.

During the reign of Queen Victoria, England became the international clearinghouse for design ideas. Carved and paneled doors, often inset with glass, were standard in the more affluent households. During the early 1900s, the door remained a prominent design feature associated with the Arts and Crafts and Art Nouveau movements. Regardless of the changes in styles in any given period, the door continued to serve as a symbol of the taste and status of the home owner.

After World War I, however, the residential door lost all resemblance to its former self. Commercially, doors continued to serve as status symbols, however. Banks, powerful brokerage firms, trade centers, and civic buildings still made use of double doors in large proportions, thus projecting not only hospitality but affluence.

Although a good door will virtually last forever, over time problems can develop, the most common of which are paint buildup and loose hinges. Generally, some minor work will correct the problems and result in an authentic older door that closes properly, swings effortlessly without slamming, and looks distinctive and beautiful.

Paint can often be removed from a door with either a heat gun or a chemical stripper. Whatever the method, it is important to follow the manufacturer's instructions.

Hinges and hinge screws often need to be tightened or replaced. If the screws have worked loose and stripped the screw hole, making the hole too big, replace the screws holding the hinge on the door with a flathead screw that is longer. The screws on the jamb side cannot be replaced with longer screws since there is usually an empty space between the door jamb and existing framing studs. In this case, a door hanger should be called; he or she will remove the door and re-drill the holes. To find a door hanger, call a local merchant who sells doors or a building engineer in a large commercial building who could refer you to a specialist in hanging doors.

If you want to buy or replace an authentic door, there are specialty reproduction door manufacturers who will provide a catalog of their historic doors and doorways. These doors come "prehung" with an assembled door jamb that has been tested to insure that the door will operate properly if installed correctly.

If you would like a custom-designed door, you will need to work with a team of craftspeople. A carver or custom mill shop can create the decorative wood elements of the door you want, and a local carpenter who specializes in door hanging could be contracted to install the door, frame, and jamb. With some research, however, you should be able to locate a door manufacturer who still takes orders for custom-made doors, including hand-carved and/or beveled and stained glass inserts. The doormaker will probably contract an artisan who works with the glass or does the wood carving. The artisan will ship the decorative piece to the doormaker who will complete the door. Though usually very rewarding in the end, this type of project requires careful planning and cooperation on the part of the homeowner, and it takes some time.

*T*he
finely crafted woodwork and
hand-rubbed appearance of the
paneling adds richness to this staircase.
The use of small rectangular insets
dates back several centuries, but was
particularly popular during the late
Victorian period (above).

*T*his
elaborate ceiling is based on the Italian
Renaissance style. The deep decorative
moldings reflect the glazed tile pattern
of the floor below. Creating a ceiling
such as this is an interesting way to
add finely crafted woodstrap work to a
room that might be too small to
support other wood treatments (left).

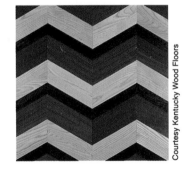

Victorians

in England preferred oak floors. An oak and walnut border in the classic Greek key pattern enhances plain oak planks (top). The rich geometric pattern of this walnut floor (above, far right) was highly valued during the eighteenth and nineteenth centuries. Brazilian hardwoods were valued for their exciting patterns (above right). Here, Kentucky Wood Floors combines ash, wenge, and padauk woods in a Herringbone pattern. This parquet floor (above) is made from cherry wood in a revival of a classic pattern called Marie Antoinette.

Floors

In the Middle Ages, flooring was usually made of stone simply because man and beast often came into the household together. The upper floors of a building were usually made from simple joined wood planks. In time, the animals were relegated to the outdoors and, although stone flooring remained a feature of the entry hall, wood became the accepted flooring for the rest of the house.

With the Renaissance, the French began experimenting with different types of flooring joinery. Furniture and flooring designs that the Italians created by using different colors of wood were perfected by the French and are now commonly known as wood inlay, parquetry, and marquetry. By the time parquetry techniques had come into vogue, the simpler pegboard and tongue-and-groove method of laying flooring was considered passé and provincial. Sophisticated flooring with an inlay of different colors of wood or wood patterns with hidden interlocking joinery became popular and was used almost exclusively in finer homes.

By the Victorian period, quarter-sawn wood flooring was generally used, with stone and marble flooring and walls in the formal areas, such as the entry. In the rest of the house, wood floors dominated as the backdrop for elegant and colorful carpets.

Today, wood flooring is enjoying a revival for the same reasons it was originally preferred to stone: it absorbs sound and has a special beauty, making it an excellent background for the other household amenities and furnishings.

Restoration of an authentic floor can be very difficult, especially when existing floorboards need to be matched. One source for the same wood can be within the house, such as from a closet floor. You can remove flooring from this area, use it for the patch work and replace the closet floor with other wood. If this is not sufficient, there are some companies that make special flooring planks and a few companies that actually specialize in maintaining an inventory of flooring, paneling, and other woods that have been removed from historic structures that have been demolished. If all else fails, contact the nearest wholesale supplier of hardwoods and ask him to provide you with the names of a few of his clients who might be able to make or match your flooring. Give the supplier an approximate square footage of the area to be replaced so that he has an understanding of whether to send you to a small operation or to a large retail flooring supplier.

Maintenance of wood flooring is very important. The floor takes a great deal of abuse from foot traffic and sliding furniture, not to mention dropped items. Since wood is a natural material, it also changes with atmospheric conditions. One of the problems facing many homeowners today is wood flooring that creaks. This is generally caused by the wood's not being properly maintained and then allowed to dry out. Correcting this problem can be fairly involved and may require the services of a flooring expert. To avoid drying out, varnish, used as a sealant, can make a significant difference. The varnish should be applied when the flooring is raw, then reapplied periodically as part of an overall maintenance program. When varnish is worn through, the floor should be sanded and revarnished to avoid problems such as creaking that can result when the wood is not properly maintained.

A floor that has been properly maintained will need to be refinished only every ten to fifteen years. If less than twenty percent of a floor is damaged, it is generally less expensive and less time consuming to sand and refinish than to replace the floor altogether.

Badly damaged wood floors generally require sanding. Although sanding machines can be rented, you may want to consider hiring a professional since the drum sanding machines can be difficult to control. Improperly handled, these powerful sanders can damage the floor by sanding the flooring down too far.

Many floors that have become dull, or are only partially worn, can be easily refurbished by thoroughly cleaning with turpentine. Use a natural bristle brush and steel wool to loosen grime and dirt, then wipe the floor with a lint-free rag. Fill any gouges or cracks, and lightly sand the filling to match the original wood surfaces. You can apply stain to the worn areas as needed, being careful to blend the color of the stain to the original floor. Use a lint-free rag to remove excess stain. Allow the floor to dry thoroughly before applying at least two coats of a clear sealer, such as varnish or polyurethane, that is compatible with the original coating.

Courtesy Kentucky Wood Floors

© Max Eckert Photography/FPG International

TONGUE AND GROOVE JOINT

Tongue and groove joinery is a method of concealed wood joinery that early craftsmen developed for use in the construction of wall panels, cabinets, flooring, and furnishings (above).

A white stain has been applied to the oak floor here, then wiped off, a process called pickling (above left). This quarter sawn oak floor is bordered with inlaid walnut (bottom left).

variation on this pierced-wood design with the shuttered window panel and louvers that they used in front of or in place of glass panes.

The lathing of wood to create decorative wood turnings has existed for centuries. In the 1700s in France and England, hand-operated tools were mounted on special workbenches and used to keep a block of wood turning. A sharp knife was then passed along the length of rotating wood blocks, cutting patterns into the wood. Later, a belt allowed the equipment to be operated with a foot pedal, and templates were used as a guide to determine when and how deep the knife should cut into the wood. With this equipment, the wood shop also produced shapes that were turned into dowels, balustrades, and newel posts that were used not only for grilles and ventilators, but also for bannisters, columns, cabinetry, and so forth.

During the Victorian era, wood ventilators were used not only to allow air to circulate but also as decorative devices to separate and define one space from another. They were often found around windows, doors, and other exterior areas, such as porches and dormers. This pierced woodwork came to be known as Victorian gingerbread and was usually made of flat wood pieces with elaborately cut-out, pierced fret pattern designs. These pieces were usually joined with glued dowels. Sometimes these brackets, ventilators, grills, and dormer pieces were also enriched with turned wood pieces and round wooden bead work.

Today, there is still a thriving industry among the specialty woodworking shops that produce turned wood shapes and gingerbread architectural decorations after the style of this bygone era. Many of these pieces are readily available at local wood molding supply houses or through catalogs published by the companies that specialize in Victorian gingerbread.

Repairing gingerbread or turned wood pieces can be another matter. To repair an original ventilator, the homeowner with some carpentry skills might enjoy taking a jigsaw in hand to try to replicate the original broken part. If, however, you lack the patience and skills required to make the piece, it is best to contact a local cabinetmaker, woodworker, or antique furniture restorer. They have the proper tools and hardwood supplies necessary to make the parts that are usually qualified to do the job. Stripping the paint and varnish to refinishing a ventilator can be very difficult, also because of the intricate grooves and corners. The simplest solution to this problem is to remove the piece and take it to a shop that has a dip tank, making the stripping an easy matter.

Turned balusters, posts, and railings are accented by the painted moldings placed under each step.

Gingerbread and Turnings

Pierced wood designs or gingerbread, are created by cutting patterns completely through the wood, thus allowing light to pass through. Patterns, often in the shapes of leaves and flowers, were used by rural Europeans as window insets, screens, or grilles, to permit the flow of air. Window insets were eventually replaced by glass. The colonists in Canada and America made use of a

© Maria Pape

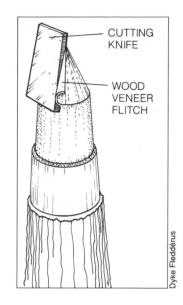

CUTTING KNIFE

WOOD VENEER FLITCH

Dyke Fledderus

Wood cut in this manner reveals grains with angular feather patterns (above). Veneer flitches, or sheets, are bundled together in sequence to make usable lumber.

Finely finished wood paneling was much favored by eighteenth- and nineteenth-century Europeans and Colonial Americans. Here, the joined wood panels and panel surrounds are combined with an exposed beam ceiling in the Tudor manner (left).

Paneling

Although it was the Norman invaders who brought wood paneling to England, the French Boissiere craftsmen gave us the advanced technology of room panel fitting and design. Much of the paneling of seventeenth- and eighteenth-century France and England was designed to fit over existing stone walls, with the panels and moldings constructed to be set in place and joined together. The seams between panels were covered with the molding and panel surrounds. Often, the paneling was as much as three inches thick, which provided structural strength and accommodated the deep carved ornamentation. The paneling was shimmed to fit into the room, and sometimes large gaps and air pockets were left between the wood paneling and the stone walls. In essence, the old masters viewed the paneled room as a room within a room, predesigned, cut, and ready to drop into place.

The artificially colored paneling available at the local homeowners building supply retailer usually bears little relationship to the wood-paneled rooms from earlier periods of craftsmanship. These thin sheets of printed or faux veneer sheets were the answer to the taste trends of the 1950s and 1960s that also included chipboard sliding closet doors. Paneling of solid hardwood or a combination of hardwood and real veneer-covered lumber core is being made today by specialty paneling companies. Lumber core is similar to modern plywood sheets except that the core is made of joined solid wood, and one side is finished with a veneer layer of the desired wood (such as walnut, oak, ash, or mahogany). A new wood product is cloth-backed hardwood veneer stock that is specially prepared to be applied with contact heat adhesives. This is called pliant wood and can be used with milled hardwood moldings, since the pliant wood material is also real wood.

Today, specialty panels are precut at the workshop to verified specifications from drawings of existing wall elevations. The panel surrounds are milled and grooved to allow for the adjustment at the job site.

The success of any architectural paneling project depends a great deal on planning. Accommodating a budget can be difficult. Hardwoods have never been cheap, and milling and installation costs also add to the total. When having work done by a specialty panel workshop, examine the wood stock they proposed to purchase to insure that it has graining that is compatible with your setting and meets your expectations. Wood is as varied as the abilities of the craftspeople who work with it.

This weathered oak paneling is highlighted by sculpted insets and crown moldings (above). The satin sheen of pickled wood is an interesting alternative to the usual high sheen of paneling.

Superior craftsmanship is evident here in the accuracy of proportion and the fine joinery of the wood paneling and fireplace surrounds. The broken pediment above the fireplace finds its origins in the Renaissance movement.

To ensure that the methods used to join the wood are commensurate with the value of the pieces, use a skilled craftsperson to handle the installation. Select a craftsperson who understands the methods of assembly for paneled rooms. Adjustments to compensate for irregular rooms (such as rooms with a slightly sloping floor) are often made at the doorways and windows—places where the "standard" shape of things is interrupted—and these adjustments are generally beyond the talents of the nonprofessional.

The finishing work, on the other hand, is a job that you may decide to do yourself. Regardless of whether you or an experienced wood finisher stains and seals the wood, be sure to acquire several extra running feet of paneling. This should be used to perform test patches of the stain and finish, including the wood filler. Wood filler is used to prevent the panels from taking the stain unevenly and can add to the refinement.

The craftsmen of bygone days usually only colored the wood to enhance its natural beauty, but this task required two different colors of stain or dye. The first coat was a lighter stain that highlighted the grains; this was overglazed with a darker stain. The woods were then carefully rubbed and polished to a marvelous lustre. This type of finish can be simulated today by using a light and dark stain combination, followed by an application of finishing oils that contain varnish resin. These coatings provide maximum water sealing while adding oil to the wood to prevent drying and excessive swelling or shrinkage from atmospheric changes.

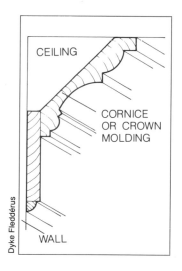

CEILING

CORNICE
OR CROWN
MOLDING

WALL

*C*ornice
*and crown moldings are sometimes
achieved by stacking two or more
patterns on top of each other to obtain
the desired height and depth. They are
often attached to an angle to conceal
the joint between the wall and the
ceiling.*

*H*ardwoods
*at Silverton Mills are carefully selected
for each specific project (top).*

*T*hese
*classic moldings bring impact as well
as careful balance to the entry hall of
the Mount Pleasant mansion in
Philadelphia (left).*

Moldings

Toward the end of the Middle Ages, as society became more sophisticated, open ceiling rafters and beams common to the times came to represent the early, more impoverished days. To eliminate these unpleasant reminders, the elite covered the beams and supports with moldings. Eventually, delicately hand-carved moldings, along with ceiling panels, completely covered beams and rafters.

Today, a similar look can be easily achieved with veneered coreboard and stock moldings. The molding industry of today often simulates the carved moldings of yesterday by first milling the shape and then applying premolded adornments made of "compo." The applied compo decoration accepts stain in the same manner as wood. Cornice moldings for draperies and bed canopies are projections of the same type as those used for ceiling cornices, carved crestings along the top of paneling, door surrounds, or furniture tops.

Whether you are running molding along beams, baseboards, windows, doors, or to finish paneling, modern technology makes it fairly easy to accommodate budget considerations. Most moldings can be ordered through supply houses and cut to the desired length. It can be effective to select two to five stock patterns of moldings that can be stacked or combined into a composition with a custom look. If you are replacing a missing piece of authentic molding and cannot locate it at a supply house, a craftsperson who can replicate the molding or a woodcarver are probably your only recourse.

Courtesy The Dahlke Stair Co.

Courtesy The Dahlke Stair Co.

TOM DAHLKE

Courtesy Tom Dahlke/photo by Michael McAndrews

Tom Dahlke combined his studies at the California College of Arts and Crafts with boat finishing. It was then that he got into the habit of taking on projects that were "way over his head," forcing himself to find solutions to difficult woodworking problems. This experience and later, time put into building energy-efficient, contemporary homes, and custom furniture and period restorations, added to his excellent background in woodworking. Finally, after observing master stairbuilder John Frano at work in Lyme, Connecticut, Dahlke settled into the business of building "just about anything anybody wanted."

Dahlke's talent and his taste for tackling tough design problems, eventually led him to establish the Dahlke Stair Company, where curved stairs are his specialty. The precise art of making a staircase calls for a special combination of engineering and sculpture talents. Dahlke uses these talents to handcraft custom wooden staircases from original designs or architectural specifications in any style, from rough hewn to Postmodern.

Whether he is building a contemporary curved stair or replicating an authentic historic staircase, Dahlke first makes all of the components in his shop, then assembles and custom fits them on site. He usually makes rails from mahogany or oak, cutting them from solid blocks of wood. He matches the grain in the pieces by cutting the wood in order and gluing it back together in the same order so that the grain patterns and color stay exactly as before. Each baluster is custom made and, although Dahlke uses advanced technology when constructing the stair rail, much of the design and finishing work is done by hand.

Dahlke is often called upon to mix old with new, since traditional stairs mix well with modern architectural design. Among his many accomplishments, Dahlke has installed Victorian stairs in new buildings; he built a staircase that extended two flights, from the basement to the second floor; and he designed and built a spiral stair for an octagonal house. His most noteworthy historic contribution is the staircase in the Standish House, which was built during the Federal period and is still standing in Wethersfield, Connecticut.

*M*aster craftsman Tom Dahlke cuts the pieces of his balustrades from solid blocks of wood. Each step in the construction of his custom staircases—from the measured shop drawings, to the joining and finishing—is done by hand. The wood balusters are turned and delicately incised with spiral rope patterns, such as those shown here, and other designs. Precise craftsmanship is required to create the curved railing of this staircase (left).

This

Victorian fireplace mantle is hand carved with specially turned wood details. Symmetrically placed urns punctuate the pediment moldings (right).

Classic

Roman fluting and acanthus leaf corbels are featured on this English fireplace front (below).

Mantles

The overmantle and fireplace surrounds started as a massive piece affixed to the chimney and evolved into a piece of furniture. In the Elizabethan period, it was carved from wood or stone with a brick or stone facing in the hearth. During the Georgian period, it featured projections and a space above the mantle area to display artwork. By the 1800s, the fireplace had been substan-

tially reduced in size, and the overmantle mirror became an important ornament and status symbol. Elaborately carved wood and gilded mirror frames remained the style for many years.

Probably the most important development in mantles was the contribution of the English designer Robert Adam, who built his creations with the classic proportions of Roman design (see page 30). Those proportions influenced the colonial fireplace mantle in the New World, which were made from planks that were precut and fitted with carvings and other moldings. The planks were sometimes fluted or incised with other patterns.

Today's mantle is a piece of furniture that is merely affixed to the wall as ornamentation for the functional parts of the fireplace. Many specialty shops make mantles by machine, but there are still a few shops that can add handcarved details. Many mantle manufacturers produce and have catalogs for easy selection, replicas of authentic pieces. Expenses often depend on the detailing you require on the mantle. A simpler mantle, obviously, would be less expensive than an ornate one. For installation, you will need to contact fireplace specialists that might include both a carpenter and a mason.

Staircases

One wood craft that is nearly extinct today is the art of custom-crafting a curved staircase. The few craftspeople who still practice this art today often have long waiting lists. This requires cutting wood with precision so that the grain matches along the entire length of the rail. Carving and finishing the parts of the staircase is done by hand, and the bannister is put together in small sections, then taken to the site for installation.

Creating a custom curved staircase today begins with a blueprint. The craftsperson may use a lamination process to adhere strips of wood onto a frame. The wood used is generally a good hardwood, since stairs and bannisters must be solidly built to withstand a great deal of traffic. Often, finishing and other custom carving work is still done by hand. Because of the time and talent required for construction, it is easy to spend more on a two-foot section of curved rail than on fifty feet of straight rail. With this in mind, it is important to collect as much

information as you can about staircase possibilities so that you have a clear idea of exactly what you want and can afford. Once you commit to the design, you cannot turn back without tearing everything out.

Repairing an authentic staircase can also be very tricky. Staircases were never built to be taken apart, and, generally speaking, there is no quick fix for major staircase problems. The nonprofessional should never attempt to take the staircase apart. Matching the wood for repairs can sometimes be a problem, as well. Chestnut, for example, was a popular wood for bannisters at one time and is almost impossible to find.

There are companies today that specialize in making bannister moldings and carry stock patterns for curved bannisters that are ready-made. Many architects and homeowners find it expedient and cost effective to plan their projects according to the shop specifications of the more readily available stock parts, which can actually be ordered through a catalog. Although this is not the same as a customcrafted curved staircase, many are very beautiful and effective.

*T*his
staircase in process has a steeper than usual ascent and a limited landing space, both challenging considerations to the builder (above). A curved staircase solved the architectural problems with balance and interest, as the finished one to the left displays.

*A*nother
design solution for a staircase with a steep ascent is to make a sharp curve at the landing (above top).

Authentic craftsmanship is combined with ingenuity in this room to provide a unique and dramatic richness. The fine cabinet work reflects an American Colonial simplification of a favorite Tudor panel design. The room is highlighted with etched glass and a hand-painted and -stenciled ceiling.

Cabinetry

Before the Renaissance, cabinetry in homes was minimal. The most important piece of furniture was a chest that could be loaded with valuables and quickly moved to escape approaching invaders. This chest doubled as seating, while the table was often converted to a bed at night. With the paneled or wainscoted room, however, came other inventions for added human comfort. These included window seats and built-in shelving to hold household records, inventories, and books. Eventually, paneling featured special projections onto which chairs made of the same wood were attached. Later, they were no longer attached to the paneling so that they could be moved.

Cabinets with doors were built to provide storage or to hide valuables from untrustworthy or official eyes. Because people at this time never knew when certain goods would be available, they often kept large inventories in these early cabinets. These goods included silks, linens, clothing, weaponry, books, food and riding equipment.

Cabinetry and paneling were sometimes decorated with marquetry or the inlay of other colored wood veneer pieces. The people of the Eastern Empire and the Moors of Spain continuously practiced this craft, which originated during the Roman Empire. In addition to wood pieces, they used ivory, metal, and shell in the inlaid patterns. Craftsmen sliced wood into veneers at different canted cuts to expose the different patterns of grain. Such pattern cuts as rotary cut, half round, and cone cut veneers were sliced from the wood stock, providing crotch graining, burl, and silver graining. These patterns are also sometimes called wavy, curl, fiddleback, blister, quilted, birdseye, and ribbon.

During the later Middle Ages, the craft guilds fostered cooperation between craftsmen, a practice that particularly befitted cabinetry. For example, a cabinetmaker would construct the basic shell of the commode or bombé chest, then a veneer finisher would add the veneer, including any lacquering or japanning. Generally, the metal ormolu was affixed and the marble top laid. Only then was the finished product, the making of which had involved three craftspeople, delivered to the buyer.

The French, always inventive furniture- and cabinetmakers, fashioned the first toilet from a porcelain chamber pot that was concealed under a carved woodenskirted seat. The mistress of Louis XIV had such a toilet cabinet, complete with gilding and the most costly handpainted decoration and ormolu. The first bathroom sinks were also devised from a wood commode that was fitted with a marble or tile top and a splash board. Originally conceived to be movable, this cabinetry eventually was attached to the wall as a permanent fixture in the bathroom.

Today, there are countless sources of cabinetry for not only the kitchen and bathroom, but also for free-standing or built-in cabinets in other areas of the house. Companies specializing in cabinetry in all types of wood and wood products and in all price ranges can replace cabinetry in almost any style and within a reasonable amount of time and budget.

Custom handcrafted cabinetry is another matter, however. It can take a craftsperson months just to create one custom piece, and the time and talent involved often adds up to an expensive project. Still, there is no comparison between some factory-made cabinetry and handcrafted work from a superior craftsperson. For this reason, some people do opt to have the custom work done. Besides the woodworking skills, find a craftsperson with the knowledge and experience to properly mount the units so that they do not pull away from the walls over the years. For bathroom and kitchen cabinetry, the counter tops need to be completely watertight as well. Similarly, the restoration of existing wood cabinets in the bathroom or kitchen should include proper resealing of the grout and tile or marble surfaces to protect the wooden underparts from the warping and swelling that can occur when the wood is exposed to moisture.

Courtesy Mountain Lumber Co.

Reclaimed wood provided by Mountain Lumber is turned into custom crafted cabinetry and beamed ceilings in this country-style kitchen (left). Notice the cathedral ceiling left open above the beams.

Finely cut and fitted cabinetry fulfills the aesthetic demands of this kitchen (below). Custom features, such as the lighting in the top shelves of these cabinets, can be added when a room is personally designed for the client.

© Bill Rothschild/Margot Green, designer

WILLIAM DRAKE OF MOUNTAIN LUMBER

Courtesy Mountain Lumber Co.

Mountain Lumber's founder, William Drake, first became interested in virgin long-leaf heart pine wood in 1974. Possibly the finest lumber ever grown, this pine bears little resemblance to pine as we know it today. Originally exacted from a very slow growing tree which took anywhere from 150 to 450 years to mature, by the turn of the century, these trees had all but disappeared, and the ecological balance needed for them to flourish had been destroyed.

Today, heart pine is a retrieved wood. Mountain Lumber locates structures constructed before 1900 that are about to be demolished and reclaims the wood. The company then resaws it so that architects and homeowners can use it for tongue-and-groove flooring, paneling, millwork, custom cabinetry, doors, exposed beams, and moldings.

Whenever possible, the company documents the history of the wood, noting the structure that it is being reclaimed from and a bit of history about that structure. Using photographs along with written notes, they catalog the wood and pass this history along to the buyer.

The dirty old timbers that Mountain Lumber drags out of historic buildings are turned into solid planks and paneling that glow with the luxurious hues of this ancient pine. To achieve this, Mountain Lumber employees first pull all of the nails out by hand. The timbers are then sawn into one- and two-inch boards and kiln dried. Finally, the rough boards are run through a molder to produce the smooth flooring, paneling, and molding that represent not only history but provide a piece of nature that is no longer otherwise available.

The wood from Mountain Lumber has come from such historic buildings as the first Gimbel's Department Store and the original Burpee Seed Company in Philadelphia. This and other historic wood from Mountain Lumber has found its way into countless contemporary residences, as well as historic authentic homes in every state in the United States, and parts of Europe. Virgin long-leaf heart pine wood can be seen in the Treasury Department and the Blair House in Washington, D.C., and the Portland Museum of Art in Portland, Maine.

Courtesy Mountain Lumber Co.

Courtesy Mountain Lumber Co.

Courtesy Mountain Lumber Co.

*M*ountain
*Lumber specializes in supplying
reclaimed pine. This outstandingly
beautiful wood is salvaged from
historic buildings about to be
demolished and reprocessed for use as
cabinetry, paneling, and flooring.*

Craftsmanship is reflected in this room in the raised panel wainscot, foliated crown moldings, and door surrounds with pediments and fluted columns (left).

Restoration Guidelines

While it is difficult to skimp on wood-crafted products without sacrificing quality and integrity, there are ways to bring the expenses down. Design requirements should be minimal; a simple pattern is obviously less expensive than a more ornate pattern. Shopping in catalogs and antiques stores will give you an idea of stock trim items, such as molding, available and patterns to copy or select from. A drawing to scale should be made of the project to avoid costly proportion mistakes, and, where possible, consider doing some of the preparation or finishing work yourself.

Next to the time and talent of the craftsperson, the cost of the wood and the tooling can be the biggest budget considerations. Elaborate tooling requires a substantial amount of setup time, so most larger workshops are reluctant to do custom work or to cut less than a 1,000 feet of any particular pattern at once. However, if you need a specialty pattern made, call the closest wholesale hardwood supplier and ask for a referral to a custom mill shop. These independent shops bear the production cost of the finished piece, which may include subcontracting work out to a specialist who grinds knives to make the proper tooling for the project. Once a steel knife has been ground, it usually has to be tempered at a foundry. The time involved to design, make shop drawings and specifications, create custom tooling (when necessary), and the tooling setup time alone can make a small, custom job very expensive.

Nevertheless, a floor, door, paneling, staircase, or cabinet made from a good wood by a qualified craftsperson should provide you and future generations years of service and beauty. The finished product will reflect the patience and care contributed by the craftsperson in a way machine work never can.

This entry hall demonstrates the typical Georgian style, with painted paneling, columns, and a grand staircase (above).

This curved wooden staircase, framed by the Georgian style arched doorway, is the focal point in the entry of the Woodruff House in Macon, Georgia (far left). Stacked moldings above the arch and classic columns provide support.

PLASTER

Plaster craftsmen have been practicing their trade since at least 4000 B.C. The ruins of ancient Mesopotamia reveal that the plasterers of early civilizations had already begun sculpting and shaping plaster for architectural ornamentation. By 2000 B.C., the plaster craftsmen had advanced their skills to include incised fret work, low relief work, and other decorative arts. The ruins of the Palace of Knossos (1500 B.C.) on the Island of Crete indicate the richness in which plaster was colored, decorated, and painted with sculptured bas-relief figures and other decorative symbols.

Similarly, the application of stucco has a rich history. When the Romans entered the British Isles, their chroniclers noted that the Celtic tribes had made their huts in a forked post-and-beam type of construction that was similar to the huts that they had seen in Germany. The Celts interwove the spaces between the posts and beams with branches,

*T*he
decorative plaster strapwork ceiling in
this room accentuates the woodwork
and serves as a formal backdrop for
the chandelier (right).

*T*he
technology and craft of precast stone
and plaster ornamentation is centuries
old. Here, in the City Hall in Rochester,
New York (previous page), modern
materials are combined with
craftsmanship to create rosettes
and a portrait medallion
set in a field of oak leaves.

wicker, and bark. This supporting wall structure was then filled with mud, which was sometimes covered with a coating of clay, making it more resistant to moisture. (This ancient process is remembered today, when some plaster craftspersons and stuccoists refer to themselves as "mudders.") This particular construction eventually evolved into a permanent architectural style that was used in the half-timber and half-stucco structures of the Tudor period. Later modified to include brick-filled walls, the Tudor style has prevailed throughout history from these humble beginnings.

While there is some evidence that the Celtic tribes may have known the techniques of cementing stones together, this practice was probably not used much when the Roman legions entered the British Isles. During their time there, however, the Romans built stone docks, battlements, warehouses, and an extensive typical Roman villa, which became the foundation of London. However, the Italians of the Renaissance provided the English plaster craftsmen with the fundamentals of the plaster arts, including formulas and tools, from which the decorative relief elements of ceilings, walls, and stairways of the Palladian, Victorian, and Edwardian homes were created and flourished.

Since the secrets of Roman craftsmen were buried under the rubble of the war and social upheaval that followed the end of the Roman Empire, the artisans of Renaissance Italy had to rediscover the preparation formulas, tooling, and techniques of the earlier masters of this craft. Through study of fragmented ruins and experimentation, the Italians learned that their Roman forefathers had used up to eight coats of stucco and plaster, often varied in grade and quality. The foundation wall was usually made of sun-dried brick, stone, or other masonry fill, and was generally covered with rough stucco, over which another several layers of plaster were applied. The final coat applied was a special plaster that had powdered white marble added to it. It was carefully blended to slow down the setting time to allow the master to model and sculpt the damp plaster into a low-relief decoration. This formula and method for producing powdered white marble plaster decorations was used by all of the master craftsmen for the next 300 years.

Throughout the generations, master plasterers have continued to use almost the same techniques, whether they were designing and constructing a cartouched painted wall for a pharaoah's tomb, a grand staircase for a chateau, or a fireplace frieze for a Palladian manor house. However, instead of seven or eight layers, the craftsmen of England and France normally used only up

© Steve Nichols

to five layers for their walls, and that included in situ modeling and other ornamental plaster compositions that adorned the walls. For the construction of a wall and ceiling, a supporting structure was the obvious first step. This was usually made of wood-beam framing with the spaces filled with twigs or reeds. (This was later replaced by lath—wood strips nailed to the posts). A rough coat of stucco was applied over these filled walls, followed by an application of up to three coats of smooth sand mortar. These stucco coatings were then refined with the addition of several coats of gypsum. Only after this careful preparation was the luxuriant white marble dust mixture applied and rubbed to a smooth, polished surface.

Some historians believe that the use of gypsum and lime-based stucco and mortar for cementing materials together is as old as man's use of fire. Lime is extracted from limestone and, like marble, is a calcium-based crystal. Because it is so caustic, it is treated with water before it can be used, a process known as "tempering." In fact, ancient Roman law forbade the use of lime until it had been stored for three years and had absorbed enough moisture to make it less corrosive. After lime is tempered, it is heated, causing a chemical reaction, so that when water is added again, strong bonding crystals re-form into a hard surface. This entire process is important, since the

This plaster niche is decorated with handcrafted foliations, bead work, shell relief, and painted panels (above).

© Steve Nichols

The
painted insets of this plaster coffered
ceiling are framed with a Greek key
design and elaborate foliated
strapwork combined with egg and
dart and other patterned moldings.

use of improperly treated lime in mortars can weaken the structure to the point of collapse.

Gypsum is found in abundant quantities in natural deposits around the world, from the capitals of ancient China to the Mayan cities of Central America. Throughout ancient civilization, this material has been used in the construction of buildings from ritual gathering places to governmental seats of power. In later years, a very fine grade of gypsum was found in the Montmartre section of Paris, France. This highly regarded product became known as "plaster of paris" and has been used as a trade standard ever since.

In the French court of the eighteenth and nineteenth centuries, the official architectural styles became rigidly classical and scaled mostly for display, with little relevance to the artistic expressions of the French people. The English often criticized the court art of the French as frivolous and without meaning, and, indeed, the French court styles were often obsessively grand, with the rooms designed only to impress. However, the French craftsmen eventually developed their own style outside court edict which became known as French Provincial.

During the Queen Anne, Georgian, and Victorian periods, the plaster craftsmen of England, on the other hand, reached levels of artistic expression, elegance, and expertise that are not likely to be repeated. While both the French and the English plaster craftsmen received their knowledge and training from the master craftsmen of Renaissance Italy, the English court's artisans were guided by the love for nature developed from their Celtic ancestors. So, when the British began practicing this Italian trade, they combined classical themes with conventionalized Celtic motifs, heraldic foliations, and the lattice-and-strap work that often accompanies those designs. In this way, they set the English plaster work apart from the work of other plaster craftsmen.

This ancient Celtic design heritage of natural themes as well as of wicker intertwinings and basket weaves, continued to influence English architectural design throughout the ages. The Celtic motifs gave birth to the unique British Gothic styles, as the English steadfastly adhered to their traditional concepts. Even in the Rococo period, which exalted new and fanciful architectural ideas, the English craftsmen stayed for the most part with the traditional styles that were representative of their own history.

Ultimately, these British architectural styles and methods established themselves as major trends in the Canadian and American colonies. Many homes built in the northernmost American colonies adopted the original floor plan of Celtic cottages as the basis for the "log

cabin." The original floor plan for this cabin featured a single utilitarian room with a fireplace at one end. This eventually developed into a more advanced plan with two living spaces with a fireplace in the middle of the structure. Since wood was plentiful in the colonies, these structures were built from fallen trees, with mortar between the logs. Eventually, settlers of the new continent imported skilled plasterers from the motherland to construct their houses and public buildings and the basic cabin gave way to more modern homes.

As the demand for plaster ornamentation increased in eighteenth-century Europe and America, craftsmen experimented with several different methods and techniques to meet the need for a more efficient production of sculptured plaster decoration. New formulas were introduced to slow down the drying time of the plaster even more, for the compositions the craftsmen were modeling were increasingly demanding and elaborate. English craftsmen, like the French, were using the Roman technique of first constructing a supporting framework for the plaster with attached armatures made of wood, wooden pegs, metal wire, or nails. These were then usually wrapped with animal hair or thread to prevent the iron from staining the plaster. These armatures, also known as nailing boards, were designed to support the first coat of rough plaster until it set and formed the foundation for sculpting the low relief sections of the decorative plaster ornamentation. As in earlier techniques, this decoration was carved from a finish coat to which white marble dust had been added.

Another technique used by the nineteenth-century craftsmen dates back to the sixteenth-century Italians, who poured plaster into a wood mold. The craftsman would dust white marble powder or talc over the reverse hand-carved mold before pouring the plaster, preventing the wet stucco from sticking to the wood mold permanently. Occasionally these molds would be made from soap or hard wax and reinforced with hair, hemp, or linen. Generally speaking, however, the wood molds were preferred since they lasted much longer than, and did not have to be repaired as often as, the soap and wax molds. After these precast plaster decorations were made, they were wet-plastered to the wall or ceiling.

The eighteenth-century technique of hollow molding made the Baroque creations of Europe possible, as well as the proliferation of ornamentation in the Victorian movement. With this precasting technique, a model was first sculpted in clay or stucco, then a coating of a gypsum and stucco mixture was poured over the model to make a mold. The inside of the mold was usually soaped (to

*C*omposition
or "compo" moldings were originally developed in France. These patterned moldings are examples of some of the classic architectural designs available today (above).

*H*ere,
traditional wooden pilasters and moldings are combined with decorative plaster moldings and ornamentations, frieze panels, and crown moldings. This French-style ballroom is in the Nottoway Plantation Manor House in Louisiana (left).

serve as a releasing agent later) and a semi-liquid plaster was poured into the mold. The mold was quickly affixed to the ceiling or wall and held in place by timber stays, which were extended from the scaffolding until the casting set properly. After the molding was set, it was split and removed. Finally, it was touched up where bubbles might have formed, and the detailing was reiterated with sculpting tools.

Still another important technique used by the nineteenth-century plaster craftsmen was stamped stucco decoration. With this method, the damp plaster was applied to the wall, then stamped in situ with the desired design. Although the wooden stamp mold was commissioned from a mold carver, in this particular technique, only patterns that did not have undercuts could be used. Some of the acceptable patterns for this process were egg and tongue, garlands, leaves, frets, diapers, and rosettes. With this method, the final layer of wet stucco paste was

pressed against the wet plaster, stamping the design onto the surface. Because this was such a time saving technique, it quickly gained favor in the production of often-used moldings.

By the 1850s, mold makers had introduced gelatin molds that were flexible and permitted easy casting of sculpture in the round, as well as in heavily indented plaques. Additionally, mold makers in Scotland began to make rough castings to simulate in plaster the texture of carved stone. By 1890, these techniques were being used to produce concrete reinforced with steel for window trims, doorways, columns, and entablatures. By the time of the Paris Expo in 1900, the precast trades of Europe, Canada, and America were alive and flourishing. The revival of architecture in the Grand Manner and the coming of the Beaux Arts designs of the French and classic Baroque styles ultimately served to industrialize craftsmen of the Victorian period.

KONSTANTIN ROSENBLYUM

Courtesy Konstantin Rosenblyum

© Larry Schenker

Russian émigré Konstantin Rosenblyum began his career as a plaster craftsperson by earning a degree in architecture in the Soviet Union. There, the study and apprenticeship in many of the decorative arts, including plasterwork, is a requirement for the degree, and it was through this avenue that Rosenblyum was first exposed to the craft that would become his career specialty. Working after gradua-tion in the palaces of culture in Moldavia, Odessa, and Leningrad, he perfected the art of plaster restoration, sculpting,and mold-making that he would eventually bring with him to the United States in 1980.

Stopping for a short time in Italy, where he spent time making plaster patterns and molds, Rosenblyum gradually made his way to America. In the States he discovered that, because of his architectural background, he could easily pro-vide architectural plaster designs for contemporary as well as restoration pro-jects. He also discovered that American restoration projects were simple com-pared to the far older and much more elaborate buildings he had worked on in Leningrad. The concept of mixing the old with the new posed no problems for Rosenblyum, either, since even in the Soviet Union he was often called upon to create ornate, historically styled ceilings for newer buildings.

It is this old and new mix that represents the major portion of the work that Rosenblyum's California-based firm, K & M Architectural Designs, Inc., now takes on. While he still does restoration work for commercial as well as residen-tial clients, he has been keeping busy with an explosion of requests from major hotels in Las Vegas and Atlantic City to create often contemporary yet classical plaster work on a massive scale. In America today, it is not unusual for even the most modern building to include fluted columns and classically designed capi-tals that complement their contemporary design scheme. So, as well as in several palaces of culture in the U.S.S.R. and a smattering of restoration jobs in the United States, Rosenblyum's versatile and very high quality plasterwork can be seen in a plethora of popular hotels, including several Hilton hotels and the Crys-tal Ballroom of the Beverly Hills Hotel.

Konstantin
Rosenblyum's marvelous talent for adapting classic styles to contemporary settings can be seen in the plasterwork of this fireplace surround and mantle (right). The columns present a beautiful focal point in the archway (above).

The

French grand manner was relaxed in Colonial America. However, decorative plaster moldings, painted wood archways, window moldings and surrounds, and columns were favorite details (above right).

This

fireplace is framed by Georgian style columns with an inset oval mirror. The wide flat window sashes are also Georgian (below).

Restoration Guidelines

Today, there are many companies that are still making plaster ornamentation. One method favored by craftspersons today is to use factory mixed gypsum reinforced with flexible fiberglass cloth which replaced the hemp and animal hair plaster used during the eighteenth and nineteenth centuries. These precast moldings can be purchased from catalogs, are extremely lightweight, can be nailed into place or applied with construction adhesives or cement, and then cut to specifications by the buyer or installer.

When planning your plaster installation, be sure to measure carefully. The master craftsmen of yesteryear drew a full-scale model directly onto the walls and ceilings of the space they were decorating before they started to work. In this way, they knew exactly where each leaf, twig, cherub, and scroll would go and what size it would be. Craftspersons today still draw the basis of the work directly on the surface, but more often, a drawing of the room is made to scale on graph paper. Measure carefully when ordering from a catalog, and allow some extra length, since there will be some loss of material when the corners are cut and mitered. Once the castings are ordered, a carpenter, mason, or handyman can often handle the installation.

The condition of authentic plasterwork in older homes today should be carefully assessed before any new work begins. Sometimes original work that looks as if it needs to be completely replaced requires only a simple cleaning to be almost as beautiful as it was originally. On the other hand, the original work may be so deteriorated that extensive replication by a craftsperson is the only solution. In any event, have a professional help you evaluate the condition of any existing work as the first step.

A thorough cleaning may breathe new life into old plaster (that has porous interior core, dense water-resistant exterior), an important consideration when handling plaster walls or decorative ornamentations. If the thin, protective layer is broken or penetrated, the structural integrity of the plaster is immediately jeopardized. Because of this, it is important to avoid abrasive cleaning methods. This is true even when cleaning exterior surfaces of plaster, stucco, mortared stone, and fired brick, or the mortar between the stone and brick of fireplaces, walls and walkways.

Extreme care should be taken when selecting the cleaning method to be used, since endangering the outer layer can ultimately result in extensive damage that requires total replacement of the mortar or plaster surface. This would create an unnecessary expense.

Water, one of the elements so necessary to the formation of plaster and stucco, is also its worst enemy. The reason is that, as water passes through plaster, it begins to soften and dissolve the very minerals it had originally helped fuse together. The water moves through the body of the plaster wall, ceiling, or molding, and when it reaches the other side, it evaporates into the air, leaving mineral salts behind on the plaster surface. In the first stages of deterioration, these are seen as water stains. If the water is permitted to continually permeate the plaster, the result is a breakdown of the plaster, evidenced by

© Louis Sahuc/Stock Options

Hans Wendler/FPG International

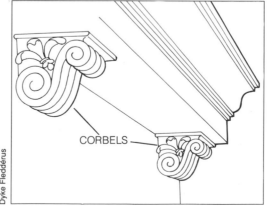

Dyke Fleddérus

CORBELS

*Corbels
(near left) were originally architectural
bracings, but they became highly
ornamental during the Roman Empire.
They were frequently used during the
Georgian and Colonial periods to add
importance to overdoor pediments,
window moldings, ceiling beams, and
exterior roof eaves.*

*The
ribbon with foliation motif became
popular in England during the time of
Robert Adam (far left).*

Courtesy David Flaharty

This plaster ceiling medallion, created by David Flaharty, is composed of historic foliated motifs and strapwork (right).

Reproduction French moldings made from "compo" castings were used to decorate the walls of this newly constructed period room by J.P. Weaver and Company (below).

© Fritz Taggart/J. P. Weaver

white chalky deposits on the plaster surface. These deposits, called efflorescence, represent the final stages of plaster deterioration. At this point, the plaster is usually considered terminally ill, and generally requires removal and complete rebuilding or replacement of the plaster surface.

The standard restoration technique for walls with minor deterioration is to first identify the source or cause of the problem. This is sometimes tricky, for water does not necessarily travel in a straight line. For example, in one unusual case of plaster damage, the problem was created by a roof soffit that had been constructed on a level plane rather than on a slant away from the house. Consequently, when it rained, the rain water ran off the roof, planed across the flat surface of the eave soffit and into the walls. It then ran down the interior walls, through the second floor flooring, and eventually accumulated in the center of the ceiling in one bedroom and the dining room. Since only a portion of the soffit was not adequately tilted upward, the damage was random, and identification of the source of water was difficult.

It is almost always necessary to call in a qualified craftsman if damage is extensive and the origin of the damage is not clear. After the source of water is determined, plaster in the first stages of deterioration is usually easily repaired by scraping the existing plaster surface with a wire brush or another tool until the damaged surface is removed and a sound base is reached. This is followed by the application of an appropriate patching compound to the brushed and dampened plaster. As mentioned earlier, plaster surfaces that are in the advanced stages of deterioration require more extensive work. The plasterer will probably need to remove the deteriorated plaster, down to the support posts or beams. Wire mesh or other lath are replaced or installed prior to the application of the first rough coat of plaster. Then, basically the same process is used for rebuilding the section that needs to be replaced as is used to create a new plaster wall, ceiling, or decorative crown molding.

Where decorative plasterwork has been severely damaged, one cost-effective solution is to remove the decorative piece altogether, then either replace it with a simple casting, or elect not to replace the casting at all, focusing instead on other areas of decorative plasterwork that might be more economically salvageable or replaceable. If you choose to replicate a special decorative piece of plasterwork that is not available in precast form, then naturally you will have to hire a craftsperson to execute and install the designed or replicated piece. Installation is very important, and the experience of the person you hire is

Courtesy J. P. Weaver

Compo
is an appliqué molding. When beated,
it is flexible and can be band-molded,
then glued to flat or curved surfaces.
Here, the delicately decorated ceiling by
J.P. Weaver and Company is
illuminated by a modern
cone light molding (left).

almost always reflected in the consistency and evenness of the installation. Be sure you pay attention to this when you are reviewing examples of his or her work.

Classic proportions can be an important issue when adding architectural details to a room, and some of the tricks employed by the masters of the past are also useful today. For example, if the ceiling is a little low and you would like it to appear higher, use a slightly higher base-board with a shallower crown molding. Also, by lowering the height of the wainscoting slightly, you will make the room seem taller and, therefore, it will appear much larger than it actually is.

No matter which method you select to incorporate the plaster design into your interior, plaster today offers the best of the past and the present. For, while the bleak drywall housing that was erected so quickly to satisfy an increasing demand for inexpensive housing is recognized for its lack of interest and overall sameness, the materials now used in modern construction are easily manipulated and adapted to restoration or recreation of the more varied interiors of the past. The art and design of plaster architectural decorations has been passed down through the ages and incorporated with modern methods to serve both the aesthetic and the practical senses today.

This intricately sculpted plaster ceiling medallion by David Flaharty features Greek acanthus leaves with foliations and rosettes in a wave pattern (below).

Courtesy David Flaharty

Courtesy David Flaharty

DAVID FLAHARTY

By 1971, sculptor David Flaharty was associate professor of sculpture and chairman of the sculpture department at a university. Then, his chance meeting with classical architect Edward Vason Jones proved to be the turning point in Flaharty's career. Jones signed Flaharty onto his team of craftspeople who were working on the Diplomatic Reception Suite of the State Department in Washington, D.C., as an ornamental plasterer.

Since then, Flaharty has contributed to an impressive array of historic projects. He designs, manufactures, and installs ornamental ceiling centerpieces and cornices. Favoring designs from the Federal and Greek Revival periods in American architecture, he uses contemporary molding materials along with his hand sculpting talents to fashion his elaborate ornamentations. Often sculpting each leaf or other detail by hand, he produces a customized piece of architectural art. In this manner, he creates and/or replicates authentic designs, always bearing in mind modern requirements, such as accommodation for electrical connections.

Concerned that with each generation the level of the skill required of authentic craftspeople is ultimately reduced, Flaharty concentrates on being the best possible practitioner of his art. He enjoys creating each ornament, he says, for the sake of art, history, and for the "sake of my own eyes." Flaharty's own home is a log cabin outfitted with an authentic Empire dining room.

Flaharty's work can be seen in a countless number of historic places, including, in Washington, D.C., the Diplomatic Reception Suite in the State Department and various rooms in the White House, and, in New York City, various period rooms in the American Wing of the Metropolitan Museum of Art. Many historic homes in the United States feature his craftmanship, including Gracie Mansion in New York City, the Roper House in Charleston, North Carolina, and a house called Rattle and Snap in Nashville, Tennessee.

Craftsman
David Flaharty applies plaster
ornamentation to a ceiling medallion,
one leaf at a time (left).

Two
of master craftsman David Flaharty's
handcrafted ceiling medallions (below).
The one to the left is decorated with
foliations, rosettes, and a border of
highly stylized leaves. Right, this
medallion has layered foliations and
bead work.

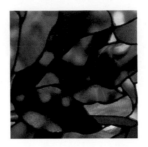

GLASS

There is evidence that glass was born before recorded history. The ancient Egyptians covered their windows with matting, cloth, or animal hides, while glass, which they considered a very valuable commodity, was used primarily for ornamental jewelry. In fact, at one point in ancient Egypt, glass beads had the same monetary value as precious gold.

One of the earliest technical applications of glass was as a glaze over clay and porcelain mixtures, creating tiles and mosaics. The Romans borrowed knowledge from the Egyptians to produce their own ornamental objects and vessels, and eventually the Roman glass makers' wares also became so elevated in status, that glass drinking vessels became more valuable than those made of either gold or silver. Like the Egyptians, the Romans used metal oxides to color their glass, adding significantly to its value as well as its beauty.

Courtesy Salvatore Polizzi Studios

As glass increased in value, the Roman government decided to tax the craftsmen for their products. Subsequently, many craftsmen left Rome, and bands of fugitive glass makers as well as other middle-class craftsmen took refuge in what were then the salt marshes of Venice. Not accessible by land, and surrounded by virtually unnavigable swamp waters, the craftsmen were protected from the tax collector, the ravages and consequences of war, and the famine and plagues that were sweeping Italy. Here, their craft developed and they flourished, so that by A.D. 1200 the glass makers of Venice were divided into two groups: those who made windowpanes and those who created glass objects of art.

Meanwhile, throughout Europe, other glass makers of the fifth century began to take refuge in isolated abbeys to escape the wars that were ravaging Europe. They began to adorn the major cathedrals with brilliantly stained glass windows. Although many of these cathedral windows are no longer in existence, a wonderful glass window dating from the ninth century still stands in a cathedral in Dijon, France.

While no one really knows who first discovered glass, it was the Egyptians who refined it and brought it to a usable art form. Their original technique for glass making was used for many centuries. First, sand was mixed with soda and ash. These elements were heated into a molten mass called "metal." The metal was then either formed into a rod for making vessels or dropped onto a surface and pounded with a wooden mallet into a flat "pane" of glass, which would later be scored and broken into the desired size and shape.

Early craftsmen also discovered that pressing pieces of glass against a rotating sandstone wheel would create a beveled or prismed edge on the glass. This edge would reflect light and create sparkling colors, not unlike gemstones. These faceted and beveled pieces of glass were normally used for candelabra and chandeliers, though small pieces were also used as ornamental inserts in leaded glass window panels. Craftsmen originally used wads of wool felt and a pumice or putty substance to polish the glass. This time-consuming practice continued for hundreds of years.

Windows did not come into widespread use on the Continent because, like the Greeks and Romans of the past, the Spanish, Italians, and French of the Middle Ages were constantly at war. Therefore, the need for secure battlement walls meant the elimination of windows. However, the English did not suffer the same recurring assaults. This, coupled with a love for light, allowed them to develop large, leaded windows. In fact, as in the

*T*be carved rosettes of this Victorian style wooden door are further enriched with leaded glass view panels that have been elaborately etched and beveled. *(far left).*

*M*odern craftsmanship is frequently called upon to restore and replace the stained glass windows of the past. This is a stained glass cathedral window set in stone *(above left).*

*H*ere master art-glass maker, Salvatore Polizzi, displays the precision of the art of lead caming. The complex design is adapted from ancient Egyptian motifs *(left).*

*T*be age old technique of fusing colored glass together with lead strips is artfully recreated in this contemporary stained glass panel by the Polizzi & Mouacdie Studio *(page 119).*

The use of *heraldric medallions was a result of the influence of the Spanish Renaissance in England. The motif is evident in this contemporary window of hand-stained glass in a stylized, foliated border. The detail above shows the intricate workmanship of lead caming and beveled glass.*

Roman Empire, large windows became so popular that the Crown created a "window tax" in 1696, which was increased many times until it was repealed in the 1850s.

The agents of the Crown also discovered that, like the ancient Egyptians, the North American Indians considered brightly colored glass beads valuable items for trade and were willing to swap large tracts of land for these—to the Europeans—common baubles. To monopolize this lucrative bartering system with the unsuspecting Indians, the English secretly built the first glass factory in the Jamestown Colony and began making trade beads in the New World. Though they tried to expand their business to include the manufacture of windowpanes, the glass makers of Jamestown were not wholly successful. The demand for glass for windows in the New World was generally very limited because the Puritan settlers, who were the same religious zealots of "Cromwell's England," had taken to destroying colored glass windows in churches as "unchristian." Instead, the colonists continued to use oiled paper, animal skins, and wooden shutters as window covers. Eventually, the Indians discovered that the beads had no value, and Jamestown was attacked and burned.

Nevertheless, as Europeans began to hear about the vast riches of the New World, the original English glass makers were followed by Dutch, Germans, and Italians. Shortly after the American Revolution, the first acknowl-edged glasshouse for making windows was established in 1803 in Boston. Two of these glass factories burned, however, and as late as 1825, European newcomers to the New World were still advised to bring their own glass panes with them on the crossing. The English brought with them a multitude of window panes and window construction methods that had been fostered by their love of light and windows. The English probably designed more window styles than any other culture in Europe, and one of their favorite designs was the bow window, which had been conceived in pre-Elizabethan times. This window is basically an outward window with three sides, and originally was composed of a number of small inset panes of leaded glass. Often accompanied by a window seat directly under the window, this original English design was to be adapted in different forms in the Americas from that time until well into the twentieth century.

During the Victorian period, the technology of glass making advanced dramatically as many new innovative patterns and techniques were created. It was during this time that etched, or engraved, windowpanes became popular. Like beveled glass, etched patterns result when glass is pressed against a rotating abrasive wheel. Originally, glass etchers used finely tooled copper or sandstone wheels attached to lathes. The glass was suspended from a beam to counterbalance the weight, and the craftsmen were able to manipulate it to create the desired pattern.

Glass
panels etched with an elaborate
landscape are set into an arched wood
door for a stunning example of
authentic craftsmanship used in
contemporary design.

Modern
etching and glass polishing techniques
enable craftsmen to create complicated
fluid designs, such as this water nymph
by Kensington Glass Arts (above).

Etched
mirrors and glass in the Art Deco style
are incorporated into this
contemporary bathroom (right).

Etched Glass

Today, acids can be used to achieve similar etched effects. Special rubber liquids, or resists, are painted on the glass surface, with the desired pattern area left exposed. The glass is then submerged in a bath of acid until the pattern portion of the glass is eaten away. The acid process is hazardous, however, so it has gradually fallen out of favor with many of today's glass engravers. Instead, they will often use sandblasting, which is generally more cost effective than engraving by hand. This method employs a high pressure stream of air and sand as the abrasive medium. A stencil is cut to represent the desired pattern, and the exposed section of the stencil pattern is held under the air stream longest so that the glass becomes "etched" with a frosted surface. The texture of the frosted surface can be varied by using different grades of sand grit during the process.

The disadvantage of using either the acid etching or the sandblasting method for glass engraving is that the glass does not have the "brilliantine glitter" that was achieved by the old master craftsmen. Although the treatment and design can be expertly executed and effective—the glass work during the Art Deco period is a good example of the success of these methods—the glass will not have the same luster and luxuriousness of the original method. However, many glass engravers today will use the sandblasting method for people who want the look of etched glass but cannot afford the actual etching process. There is a significant visual difference between the two methods, and careful consideration should be given not only to budget considerations, but to this difference in appearance. If the window is going to occupy a prominent space, with lots of light reflection, it might be better to wait until a hand-engraved window becomes affordable. To make the decision easier, look at windows done by both methods, consider the placement of the window, and last, but certainly not least, incorporate budgetary considerations.

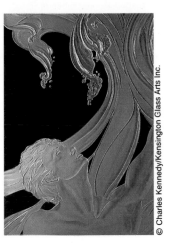

*E*tched
glass accents the marble in this modern
bathroom (left). This profile is another
example of the superior etching work
done by Kensington Glass Arts (above).

Courtesy Robert Stewart

ROBERT STEWART

One of the few craftspeople in the United States who still does large-panel engraving and etched-glass window restoration, Robert Stewart took up the craft in 1975 after he visited an exhibit of engraved and cut glass from around the world at the Art Institute in Chicago, Illinois. At that time, etching and beveling were not trades that were taught formally, so Stewart set about researching the craft and the machinery required. Pulling together sketchy information from conversations with a seventy-four-year-old glass beveler and a rough drawing he gleaned from a tattered antique English book on glass, Stewart replicated the original balance beam, known as the steelyard, and installed it in his shop. Using wood wheels that he handcrafted from poplar, along with an original sandstone wheel made in Newcastle, England—and one of his prized possessions—he concentrated his creative impulses on floral engraving. In a method similar to brilliant cutting—deep etching a pattern in glass to brilliantly reflect light—Stewart uses his specially designed machinery, along with a modern aluminum oxide wheel, to make modern pieces that complement the antique.

Stewart is committed to keeping the art of glass engraving alive, and he is generally available and willing to answer questions posed to him in the mail or by telephone. His small company, B & B Glass (so named for himself, Bob, and his wife, Barb), offers detailed instructions on how to clean antique etched glass. Old glass often develops a "patina" from the grime buildup over the years, so to anyone who requests it, he recommends grinding down one layer by hand rather than using chemicals, which he feels all too often produce an uneven effect.

Since most people have no idea what they have until it is broken and needs to be replaced, Stewart's talents and expertise in the restoration and replication of etched and engraved glass is sought by people from all walks of life. Stewart recently replaced the missing and broken 100-year-old glass panels in the Golden Dome building of Notre Dame University in South Bend, Indiana. To do this, he photographed the intact panels and used enlargements to replicate the pattern. His glass work in private homes includes numerous historic sites, such as the childhood home of Alexander Graham Bell. The Illinois Arts Council has slide files and written documentation of his technique, and the governor of Illinois was so taken with Stewart's original glass technique that he arrived with his entourage in a helicopter at Stewart's home so that he could observe Stewart's engraving technique firsthand. The governor later presented one of Stewart's pieces to the president of the United States as a gift.

Courtesy Robert Stewart

Craftsman
Robert Stewart used Victorian-style
patterns and authentic frosting
techniques to create these etched
glass panels.

Stained Glass

Modern stained glass techniques enjoy a similar integration of the past and the present. Although the use of the bars and soldered lead strips to hold the pieces of colored glass together is still used today, advances in technology have, in some cases, diminished the brilliance and jewellike sparkle of stained glass panes of the Middle Ages. Because each section of glass is often no longer made by hand, the pieces are of uniform thickness and controlled purity, eliminating the conditions that helped give the original stained glass windows their beauty. Furthermore, one modern method used by some to simulate stained glass is achieved with a heat process that literally paints enamels, dyes, mylars, or transparent paints onto modern glass, replacing the original craftsman's method of mixing metal oxide colorants directly into the molten glass. Consequently, when light passes through the glass, it meets only a very thin layer of color. The result is that the refracted colored light is dramatically reduced.

There are still a number of glass manufacturers, particularly in Germany, France, England, and the United States, who manufacture the pervasively colored glass in various thicknesses. It is this glass that superior stained glass craftspeople work with when reproducing or restoring original glass. While these special glass pieces are expensive, the colors that emanate from them are obviously superior to the simulated stained glass produced through modern methods. Pieces created with high-quality glass are more likely to be of a quality comparable with the products of well-known manufacturers such as Tiffany.

In an effort to use authentic period glass when restoring stained glass pieces, many studios carry a full line of old glass. When a project requires replacement of pieces from a particular period, the project can be completed with the old glass on hand. The actual restoration of a stained glass piece involved disassembling the window by cutting away the old lead framing (called the "came"), cleaning and scraping the old glass to remove putty, paint, or dirt, and replacing broken or lost pieces with either authentic glass pieces or custom-reproduction pieces, closely matched to the original color of the glass. The glass is then reassembled by wrapping each piece of glass with new lead caming and soldering the caming and glass pieces back together.

A
harvest scene in this stained glass window appears above a door (above).

A
glass craftsman from Kensington Glass Arts perfects the lead caming on this window panel (left).

*C*oloration
of glass by the fusion technique is practically a lost art. It has been revived in this pane by the Polizzi Mouacdie Studio (far left).

The

French recognized that an overmantle mirror created the illusion of greater depth to a room (above).
A mirror in an ornately carved wood frame can provide as great an impact to a room as an elaborate painting (above right). Notice, too, that the walls of this room carry a lovely painted texture, created by Magic Brush, a San Francisco-based decorative painting firm.

Mirrors

Although the Venetians are credited with the invention of glass mirrors, the ancient Egyptians, Greeks, and Romans all had mirrors of polished metal, including large wall mirrors. These earlier craftsmen even attempted to cover one side of black glass with foil to serve as a mirror. Several hundred years later, the Venetians introduced the clear glass with metallic backing that we know as mirrors today.

Originally considered rare and special, mirrors were prized by the courts of both France and England. The popularity of the small wall mirror intensified in England and France with the discovery and manufacture of cast glass—large sheets of rolled (rather than small panes of hand-pounded) glass that was used exclusively for large mirrors. The French also popularized mirrors by framing

them as insets on wood panels. During this period of time, the French monopolized fine glass making and, taking after the custom of the early Venetians, bestowed titles on glass makers. A Frenchman named Robinet invented the cast glass technique that ultimately gave the world plate glass, and he was accordingly awarded a gold medal and the Baccarat Glass Company for his achievements. His method, which was jealously guarded, was to pour hot molten glass metal onto a copper sheet and roll it out with a copper cylinder. France was thus the first country to have large sheets of glass, which they used to create a monopoly in fine mirrors.

In the meantime, the English and Irish continued to perfect their glass making techniques, which included grinding flint instead of sand, resulting in a very high-quality glass called flint glass. In the 1700s, the English family, Chippendale, published their guide to furniture styles, which presented all types of mirrors with their name affixed to them. This gave an enormous boost to the popularity of mirrors in interior design, particularly in England and, eventually, the New World. The English were also busy expanding their love for windows, and by the end of the Victorian era, almost every house in England and America had a decorative window.

Many residents of the heavily populated centers of Europe were looking more and more to the New World as the only avenue left to gain new wealth, properties, and opportunities. The sons of merchants, bankers, and impoverished aristocrats immigrated to the New World and brought with them the European interior design treatments to which they had become accustomed. Paneling, mantle mirrors, and Classical Revival facades adorned the homes that began to replace the one- and two-room wood dwellings of the Puritan settlers. Glass windows and mirrors, and the craftsmanship that made them so special, became established in the New World just as they had in Europe.

Restoration Guidelines

Today, modern technology offers superior tools that enable the glass craftsperson to produce windows of greater variety and shape, including curved pieces (used in design work, such as for a flower bud in a stained glass window), which were virtually impossible during the early history of glass. When considering the work of today's glass craftsperson, be sure to examine, where applicable, the placement of the metal supports that are so essential to making a strong, self-supporting decorative window. The craftsperson's understanding of the importance of the placement of these bars can be critical to the visual success of the piece. The great masters of the past worked from full-size drawings and carefully wrought the support bars so that they became a part of the overall design scheme. At the same time, they provided the support necessary to withstand strong winds and remain watertight.

Often, all that an antique stained glass piece needs to be restored to its original beauty is a good cleaning. Experts often recommend that homeowners use sudsy ammonia or any commercial window cleaner. To avoid scratching the glass, steel wool or any other such abrasive should never be used. Instead, use a soft scrub brush or a lint free cloth. For glass that has been painted over (including windows of all sizes and skylights), the paint can be removed with regular paint thinners and removers. It is virtually impossible to remove the actual color of the old glass with these thinners, since originally the color was mixed directly into the glass.

Cost considerations can be important and, in the case of decorative glass windows, that consideration may have to include the cost of the sash, metal window framing and supports, leaded caming, and the leaded-colored glass (for the stained glass projects), along with the considerable time and talent of the craftsperson as he or she develops and executes the design.

Finally, to ensure that expectations are met, it is wise to remember that glass making, unlike painting and other architectural ornamentation, is the art of letting light pass through a colored, etched, or transparent material. The finished product will never be superior to the materials or methods employed, so if there are budget limitations, a simple leaded-glass panel, for example, with a prismed, two-color border might achieve the desired look within the necessary cost confinements.

Hand-cut, beveled, or stained glass leaded windows have been immortalized by past generations as some of the ultimate art forms used in interior design. Whatever the project—from complex, multipatterned glass pieces to simple ornamental panes—working with a craftsperson in the authentic craft of glass making can be beautiful and rewarding and can provide you with an intriguing, naturalistic work of art that can be successfully incorporated into your interior design scheme.

© Randy John Noivo

***S**tained glass portrait panels, an adaptation of the Romanesque style, embellish the elaborate plaster art of this rotunda dome (above).*

***T**he glass that makes up the face of this angel has been hand colored (left).*

***T**he artistic variety and detail within the structural integrity of the piece is an example of the inspired and unsurpassable work of a master craftsperson (far left).*

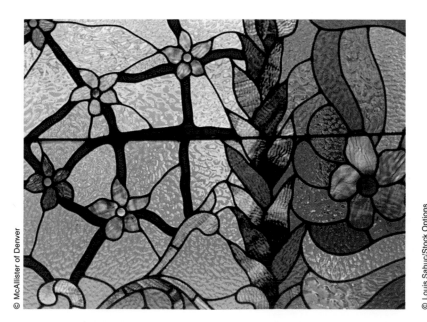

© McAllister of Denver

© Louis Sahuc/Stock Options

All of these glass designs are examples of the superior craft skills of John Salisbury and Gaytee Stained Glass.

Courtesy John Salisbury/Gaytee Stained Glass

JOHN SALISBURY

Originally founded in 1918, Gaytee Stained Glass, Inc., in Minneapolis, Minnesota has had only three owners. Owner number three, John Salisbury, began his glass career "on the bench" at Gaytee several years before he acquired the company in 1968. He now sits at the helm of this custom studio, one of the oldest in America that specializes in stained glass fabrication and restoration.

Working from a photograph or rubbing of the original stained glass window, the craftspeople at Gaytee can replicate nearly any stained glass window through a combination of modern and traditional methods. Restoration of old glass can be as simple as cleaning the glass or as complicated as matching the original design with stock from the historic glass inventory that Gaytee actively maintains. Original designs that incorporate contemporary tastes with traditional patterns are also available through Gaytee.

Stained glass windows with other problems are also referred to Salisbury. Stained glass windows with a Southern exposure, for example, may begin to bulge from the heat. Often, according to Salisbury, brace bars can be added to straighten out the window and save it for many more years to come. When done by an expert, the bars can be incorporated into the design so they do not affect the overall design of the window. For those on a budget, Gaytee often recommends setting priorities for restoration, starting with repair of the windows with the worst damage and tackling the windows with the least damage only as finances permit.

Besides repair and restoration of countless church windows, John Salisbury's Gaytee Stained Glass has worked on numerous residential projects, including the historic home of the Great Northern Railroad's founder, James J. Hill.

Courtesy Gaytee Stained Glass

G L O S S A R Y

ADOBE—A sun-dried brick made from earth.

ART DECO—A period of design in the 1920s and 1930s, that revitalized classical design.

ART NOUVEAU—A period of design at the turn of the century that featured elaborately stylized concepts.

ARTS & CRAFTS MOVEMENT—A period of design in the late nineteenth and early twentieth centuries that placed an emphasis on quality craftsmanship using natural materials.

BAS-RELIEF—Raised pattern work on a surface.

BEVELED—Edge that is cut and polished at an angle.

BUNGALOW—Style of architecture that originated in India and featured the look of a modified cottage, usually with a veranda or a porch.

CAMING—Lead metal strip material used as the structural support to hold stained-glass panels together.

CAPITALS—The decorative top or crown of a column, pilaster, pyre, or pedestal.

CHASER'S RING—A pliable pad made from pitch or resin.

COMPO—A man-made compound used as an alternative to plaster for decorative architectural ornamentation.

CORBEL—An ornamental architectural brace.

CORNICE—Crown molding; decorative molding at the ceiling line of a room, cabinet, or bookcase.

DIP TANK—A specially constructed open tank filled with chemicals and spray equipment that is used by professional paint strippers to remove paint and varnish from wood products.

ENTABLATURE—The top horizontal decorative frieze over a doorway that is supported by pilasters or columns.

FITTINGS—Decorative hardware.

FLINT GLASS—Glass that is made with the addition of crushed flint.

FORGE—Bed of coals or oven that is used to heat metal.

FRET WORK—Lattice-type work or work that features an interlocking relief pattern.

FRIEZE PANELS—Panels carved or molded in relief.

GINGERBREAD—Wood that has been cut, pierced, or incised in a design pattern.

GYPSUM—A natural mineral used to make plaster.

INLAY—The process of cutting and setting one material into another, usually in a pattern.

JAPANNING—Application of enamel or lacquer according to the Japanese styles and techniques.

JOINERY—The technology of linking two or more pieces of wood together.

LACQUERING—The application of a colored or clear coating that is made from the resin of the lac tree.

LAMINATION—The process of bonding one material to another.

LEADED GLASS—Small pieces of glass, joined by small strips of lead to form a decorative panel.

LOW RELIEF—Bas-relief work in low profile; relief work that is only slightly raised from the surface.

LUMBER CORE—A building material made with a wood core and laminated with a hardwood veneer or finish.

MARBLE FATIGUE—A state of deterioration found in marble.

MARBLEIZING—A painting technique used to simulate the look of marble.

MARQUETRY—The technique of using different types of colored wood to form a pictorial scene that is usually inlaid onto doors or cabinetry.

MASONRY—The art and technology of working with stone, brick, or concrete.

MOLDINGS—Decorative architectural detailing used as a trim or framing.

MORTAR—Bonding material used in masonry work.

MOSAIC—Small pieces of stone or tile that are inlaid to form a decorative pattern or scene.

ORMOLU—Gilded decorative metalwork.

PANEL SURROUNDS—Framework and/or moldings used to trim wood paneling.

PARQUETRY—The technique of using contrasting woods to make geometric patterns used for flooring.

PEDIMENT—A triangular or rectangular shaped entablature with cornice molding that is supported by columns or corbels and is used over doorways or at the gable end of a building.

PILASTER—A rectangular engaged column.

PORCELAIN—Fine ceramics.

POST & BEAM—A construction technique using timbers that are widely spaced vertical members (posts) that support horizontal members (beams) to form the walls of the structure and support the roof.

QUARTER-SAWN—A cut applied to wood along the radius, exposing the radial face of the wood on the cut boards.

SGRAFFITO—Incised patterns on stucco.

SMELTER—A furnace used to melt metal ore from rock.

STUCCO—A gypsum-based plaster.

TERRA COTTA—Kiln-dried red earthen clay.

TONGUE & GROOVE—A joinery system, with one piece carved to fit into the notch of a second piece, such as is found in flooring and drawers in fine cabinetry.

TROMPE L'OEIL—A painting technique used to "fool the eye" by making a flat surface take on a dimensional appearance or by making one material appear to be another.

TUDOR—An English architectural style using widely spaced timber framing with masonry or stucco walls.

VENEER—A very thin piece of wood that is usually laminated to a coarser wood product.

VICTORIAN—The period that began with Queen Victoria's reign and continued to the turn of the century.

WAINSCOT—Wood paneling that only covers the lower portion of a wall, normally stopping at chair back height.

WOOD GRAINING—A trompe l'oeil painting technique used to simulate the look of real wood.

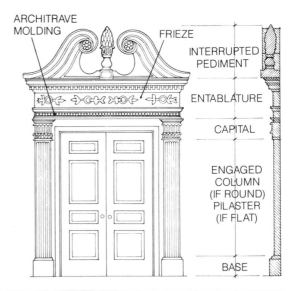

ARCHITRAVE MOLDING
FRIEZE
INTERRUPTED PEDIMENT
ENTABLATURE
CAPITAL
ENGAGED COLUMN (IF ROUND) PILASTER (IF FLAT)
BASE

Craft Associations and Guilds

Architectural Woodworking Institute
2310 S. Walter Reed Drive
Arlington, VA 22206

Canada & US member list of makers of architectural wood components.

Artisans Alliance of Minnesota
Old Chestnut Forge
6330 Lyndale Avenue
Minneapolis, MN 55423

Send SASE for list of their (member) craftspeople.

Artistic License in San Francisco
1489 McAllister Street
San Francisco, CA 94115

Send SASE for list of their (member) craftspeople.

Cast Stone Institute
2076 E. Marlton Pike
Suite 501
Cherry Hill, NJ 08003

National membership listing; information, specifications available.

Maple Flooring Manufacturer's Assn.
60 Revere Drive
Suite 500
Northbrook, IL 60062

National list of manufacturers and suppliers available.

National Oak Flooring Manufacturer's Assn.
8 North Third Street
803 Sterick Building
Memphis, TN 38103

National list of manufacturers; manual on installation, finishing, and refinishing.

National Terrazo and Mosaic Assn., Inc.
3166 Des Plaines Avenue
Des Plaines, IL 60018

List of suppliers and contractors.

Stained Glass Assn. of America
1125 Wilmington Avenue
St. Louis, MO 63111

Craft guild.

Tile Contractor's Assn. of America
112 N. Alfred Street
Alexandria, VA 22314

National membership list, apprenticeship programs, and technical data.

Tile Council of America
P.O. Box 326
Princeton, NJ 08542

National membership list of manufacturers and suppliers.

Artisans and Suppliers

Advanced Architectural Cornices
P.O. Box 17057
Arlington, TX 76017

Cornice moldings, ceiling medallions.

Danny Allessandro, Ltd.
Edwin Jackson, Inc.
1156 Second Avenue
New York, NY 10021
and
8409 Santa Monica Boulevard
Los Angeles, CA 90069

Fireplaces, mantels, and accessories.

American Architectural Art Company
1910 North Marshall Street
Philadelphia, PA 19122

Custom fabricated architectural ornamentations, sculpture, historic reconstructions.

American General Products, Inc.
1735 Holmes Road
P.O. Box 395
Ypsilante, MI 48197

Staircase systems of all kinds; all staircase detailing.

American Olean Tile
100 Cannon Avenue
Lansdale, PA 19446

Specialty tile, hexagons and borders, quarry tiles, colored grouts and other supplies.

Anthony Wood Products
P.O. Box 1081
113 Industrial Loop
Hillsboro, TX 76645

Victorian gingerbread.

The Antique Hardware Store
43 Bridge Street
Frencetown, NJ 08825

Bathroom fixtures, wrought iron and brass cabinetry and specialty hardware.

Architectural Paneling, Inc.
979 Third Avenue
New York, NY 10022

Paneling, fireplaces, mirrors, mantels, moldings.

Architectural Sculpture, Ltd.
242 Lafayette Street
New York, NY 10012

Custom ornamental plaster products.

Art Woodworking & Manufacturing Company
4238 Dane Street
Cincinnati, OH 45223

Moldings, circle head window frames, veneer paneling, casework.

Ascente
3411 C Street Northwest
Auburn, Washington 98002

Designers of wood stairs.

Atlas Mineral & Chemicals Company
Farmington Road
Meritztown, PA 19539

Corrosion-resistant mortars; setting cements in various colors.

Avonite
12836 Arroyo Street
Sylmar, CA 91342

Simulated cast stone tiles.

American Network Specialty Company
   (ANSCO)
4301 North Western Avenue
Dayton, OH 45427

Wood shutters and casement windows:
   full round, half round, double hung.

B&B Glass
Robert Stewart
6408 Hilly Way
Cary, IL 60013

Engraved glass for replication and
   restoration projects; also contemporary
   designs in etched glass.

Ball & Ball
463 West Highway
Exton, PA 19341

Reproductions of antique house and
   cabinet hardware accessories.

Barclay Products, Ltd.
424 North Oakley Boulevard
Chicago, IL 60612

Bathroom fixtures and basins.

Charles Barone
9505 West Jefferson Boulevard
Culver City, CA 90232

Distinctive wall coverings and fabrics.

The Belden Brick Company
700 West Tuscarawas
Canton, OH 44702

Decorative bricks.

Besco Plumbing
729 Atlantic Avenue
Boston, MA 02111

Authentic and reproduction plumbing
   fixtures, bathtubs, sinks, toilets, faucets;
   some that are one of a kind.

Biltmore Campbell Smith Restoration, Inc.
1 North Park Square
Asheville, NC 28801

Restoration and conservation of historic
   decorative interiors.

Bomanite Corporation International
81 Encina Avenue
Palo Alto, CA 94301

Precast concrete pavers in false stone
   finishes.

Bonsal Company
P.O. Box 38
Lilesville, NC 28091

Colored grouts, tile setting products for
   ceramics, stone and brick.

Bostik Construction Products
2930 Turnpike Drive
Hatboro, PA 19040

Color-tinted mortars, epoxy-grouts,
   adhesives.

Boston Design
100 Magazine Street
Boston, MA 02119

Designers of spiral and wood staircases.

Larry Boyce & Associates
P.O. Box 421507
San Francisco, CA 94142

Trompe l'oeil, gilding, murals, faux
   finishes, stenciling.

Bradbury & Bradbury Wallpapers
P.O. Box 155
Benicia, CA 94510

Custom-designed and hand-painted
   wallpapers.

J.R. Burrows & Company
P.O. Box 418
Cathedral Station
Boston, MA 02118

Carpet, wallpaper, and textiles for
   restoration and historic buildings.

Bybee Stone Company
P.O. Box 968
Bloomington, IN 47402

Quarry stone carving, architectural details.

Camden Window and Millwork Company
1551 John Tipton Boulevard
Pennsauken, NJ 08110

Windows, doors, and moldings.

John Canning and Company, Ltd.
P.O. Box 822
Southington, CT 06489

Traditional painting techniques:
   goldleafing, stenciling, marblezing,
   woodgraining, trompe l'oeil, and wall
   glazing.

Capitol Marble and Granite Company, Inc.
P.O. Box 1239
Marble Falls, Texas 78654

Suppliers and quarries.

Castellucci and Sons, Inc.
44 West River Street
Providence, RI 02904

Suppliers and quarries.

Chelsea Decorative Metal Company
6115 Cheena
Houston, TX 77096

Sheet metal ceiling panels and trim.

Chester Granite
Allen Williams
Algerie Road
Blandford, MA 01008

Custom stone cutting and carving,
   lettering, dressing.

Classic Ceilings
166 Waverly Drive
Pasadena, CA 91105
and
902 East Commonwealth Avenue
Fullerton, CA 92631

Relief-embossed ceiling and wall
   coverings.

CMF Colonial Moldings
17-25 Camden Street
Patterson, NJ 07503

Brass-clad wood moldings.

Colonial Restoration Products
405 East Walnut Street
North Wales, PA 19454

Wrought iron and brass hardware, wood
window sashes, doors, and doorways,
miscellaneous colonial reproduction
items.

Consolidated Dutchwest
P.O. Box 1019
Plymouth, MA 02360

Cast iron wood- and coal-burning stoves
and fireplace inserts in historic designs.

Constantine's
2050 Eastchester Road
Bronx, NY 10461

Hardware, specialty tools, and supplies.

Country Floors, Inc.
15 East 16th Street
New York, NY 10003
and
8735 Melrose Avenue
Los Angeles, CA 90069

Tiles in trim shapes, handpainted designs,
and international imports.

Cumberland Woodcraft Company
P.O. Drawer 609
Carlisle, PA 17013

Victorian millwork.

Curvoflite
205 Spencer Avenue
Chelsea, MA 02150

Supplier of architectural millwork, curved
staircases, balusters, and handrails.

Custom Castings
3324 Stuart Drive
Fort Worth, TX 76110

Fiberglass-reinforced gypsum and
concrete architectural castings,
columns, and moldings.

Dahlke Stair Company
P.O. Box 418
Hadlyme, CT 06439

Custom stairbuilder.

Decorators Supply Company
3610 South Morgan Street
Chicago, IL 60609

Plaster moldings, cornices, columns,
capitols, friezes, and mantels.

Designs in Tile
P.O. Box 4983
Foster City, CA 94404

Ceramic tiles with traditional motifs for
historic reproduction.

Devenco Products
2688 East Ponce de Leon Avenue
Decatur, GA 30030

Window shutters; colonial wooden blinds.

Diedrich Chemicals Restoration
Technologies, Inc.
300A East Oak Street
Oak Creek, WI 53154

Architectural stone and brick, and tile
chemical cleaners and sealers.

Dixie Pacific Company
Box 2296
Gadsden, AL 35903

Capitols, columns, and bases.

Driwood
P.O. Box 1729
Florence, SC 29503

Raised paneling, mantels, moldings, and
curved stairs.

Raymond E. Enkeball Designs
16506 Avalon Boulevard
Carson, CA 90746

Architectural accoutrements carved and
sculpted in solid woods.

Evergreene Painting Studios, Inc.
365 West 36th Street
New York, NY 10018

Design and execution of murals,
decorative painting, stenciling, and
restoration work.

Felber Studios
P.O. Box 551
110 Ardmore Avenue
Ardmore, PA 19003

Custom ornamental plaster products.

First Capitol Wood Products, Inc.
147 West Philadelphia Street
York, PA 17403

Aged wood for distinctive floors and
paneling.

David Flaharty
79 Magazine Road, RD 1
Green Lane, PA 18054

Sculpture and restoration of plaster
ornamentation.

Fypon Molded Millwork
22 West Pennsylvania Avenue
Stewartstown, PA 17363

Architectural details, moldings, and
pediments, molded from polymer
materials.

Gaytee Stained Glass
John Salisbury
2744 Lyndale Avenue South
Minneapolis, MN 55408

Stained glass studio designing windows for
any application; complete repair and
restoration service.

Georgia Marble Company
2575 Cumberland Parkway, NW
Atlanta, GA 30339

Supplier and quarries: slab and aggregates.

Gerber and Company
643 North Fairfax Avenue
Los Angeles, CA 90036

European hardware.

Glen-Gery Corporation
1166 Spring Street
Wyomissing, PA 19610

Decorative brick manufacturer.

P.E. Guerin Inc.
23 Jane Street
New York, NY 10014

Brass and bronze hardware.

Harden Industries, Inc.
13915 South Main Street
Los Angeles, CA 90061

Reproduction faucet systems.

Heads Up
133 Copeland Street
Petaluma, CA 94952

Oak reproduction bathroom fixtures.

T. Heinsbergen
7415 Beverly Boulevard
Los Angeles, CA

Conservation and restoration of decorative
    interiors.

Heritage Mantel
P.O. Box 240
Southport, CT 06490

Reproduction fireplace mantels.

Higgins Brick Company
1845 Elena Avenue
Redondo Beach, CA 90277

Bricks and brick paving materials.

High Brooms Details
Tom McGrath
597A Tremont Street
Boston, MA 02118

Custom bricks; terra cotta restoration.

Historic Housefitters, Inc.
Farm to Market Road
Brewster, NY 10509

Brass and hand-wrought iron hardware
    and fixtures; doorknobs.

Historic Window Shutters
P.O. Box 1172
Harrisburg, VA 22801

Hoboken Wood Floors
100 Willow Street
East Rutherford, NJ 07073

Horton Brasses
Nooks Hill Road
P.O. Box 120CH
Cromwell, CT 06416

Brass hardware and fittings.

Indian Limestone Company
P.O. Box 72
Bedford, IN 47421

Natural stone columns, friezes, arches, and
    doorways.

K&M Architectural Details
Konstantin Rosenblum
11924 Vose Street
North Hollywood, CA 91605

Restoration and custom-designed plaster
    architectural decorations of all types.

Kenmore Industries
1 Thompson Square
Boston, MA 02129

Handcrafted period mahogany doorways.

Kentucky Wood Floors
4200 Reservoir Road
Louisville, KY 40213

Klahm and Sons, Inc.
2151 NE Old Jacksonville Road
Ocala, FL 32670

Custom-designed and-crafted architectural
    metal work.

Lawler Machine and Foundry Company,
    Inc.
P.O. Box 2977
Birmingham, AL 35212
and
118 Second Avenue
Paterson, NJ 07514

Ornamental iron and metal.

Brian Leo
7520 Stevens Avenue South
Richfield, MN 55423

Custom hardware; inventory includes
    authentic and reproduction pieces.

L'Esperance Tile Works
Linda Ellett-Shore
420 Sheridan Avenue
Albany, NY 12210

Custom-designed and handcrafted tiles;
    restoration and reproduction tile work.

Mac the Antique Plumber
885 57th Street
Sacramento, CA 95819

Antique and reproduction plumbing
    fixtures and accessories; hardware.

Magic Brush Inc.
1500 B Davidson Avenue
San Francisco, CA 94124

Exterior painting restoration; interior
    painting, wood refinishing, decorator
    finishes, glazes, faux lacquer.

Marvin Window and Architectural Detail
Warroad, MN 56763

Architectural detail manual and period
    windows.

Midwest Wood Products
1051 South Rolf Street
Davenport, IA 52802

Window sashes and doors; special orders
    for reproduction.

Monumental Construction and Molding
    Company
1512 14th Street NW
Washington, DC 20005

Architectural sculptured decorative plaster,
    medallions, columns, capitols, moldings.

Moultrie Manufacturing
P.O. Drawer 1179
Moultrie, GA 31776

Cast aluminum gates, fences, railings,
plantation-style columns, outdoor
fountains, and light fixtures.

Morgan Products, Ltd.
P.O. Box 2446
601 Oregon Street
Oshkosh, WA 98164

Mountain Lumber Company
Route 2 Box 43-1
Ruckersville, VA 22968

Reclaims and resaws heart pine timbers for
use in homes and other buildings.

New England Woodturners
P.O. Box 2151
Short Beach, CT 06405

Woodturning, porch posts, columns,
newell posts, balusters, bedposts.

Norco Windows, Inc.
P.O. Box 309
Hawkins, WI 54530

Wood windowframes and doors.

N.F. Norman Corporation
P.O. Box 323
Nevada, MO 64772

Pressed metal ceilings, sheet metal
ornaments, metal roofing, shingles,
pressed metal siding.

Old House Journal
69A Seventh Avenue
Brooklyn, NY 11217

Bimonthly publication with how-to,
historic, restoration, and resource
information for homeowners.

Old Wagon Factory
103 Russell Street
P.O. Box 1427
Clarksville, VA 23927

Victorian style storm doors, ceiling
medallions, friezes in wood.

Pasternaks Emporium
2515 Morse at Westheimer
Houston, TX 77019

Victorian gingerbread trim.

Phylrich International
1000 North Orange Drive
Los Angeles, CA 90038

Lavatory and shampoo sets, porcelain
products, tub and shower sets, bidets,
wall accessories, and other coordinated
bath and kitchen hardware.

Pinecrest
2118 Blaisdell Avenue
Minneapolis, MN 55404

Metal ceilings, doors, panels, and cornices;
cast aluminum outdoor fixtures;
wrought iron oak gates, fencings,
railings, etc; also hand-carved
mahogany and oak doors.

Plasterglass
4200 North 30th Street
P.O. Box 11038
Omaha, NE

Architectural gypsum, fabrications.

Salvatore Polizzi Studio and Gallery
1065 North Fairfax Avenue
Los Angeles, CA 90046

Master glass artists for stained, beveled,
and carved glass and mirror.

ProSoCo, Inc.
P.O. Box 1578
Kansas City, KS 66117

Architectural cleaners, sealers, waxers for
natural stone, concrete, tile, brick.

Rambusch
40 West 13th Street
New York, NY 10011

Consultation, planning, design, fabrication,
installation, stained glass, metal, wood,
and lighting.

J. Ronald Reed
P.O. Box 4251 T.A.
Los Angeles, CA 90051

Conservation and restoration of decorative
interiors; historic building materials,
conservator consultant.

Reflection Studio
1418 62nd Street
Emeryville, CA 94608

Stained glass studio.

Reggio Register
P.O. Box 511
Ayer, MA 01432

Brass and cast iron grills and registers.

Rehau Plastics, Inc.
1600 Sierra Madre Circle
Placentia, CA 92670

Manufacturers of rigid polyvinylchloride
(PVC) casement windows, historic
shapes.

Restoration Works, Inc.
P.O. Box 486
Buffalo, NY 14205

Decorative hardware, plumbing, ceiling
medallions, and trims.

Royal American Wallcraft
834 South U.S. 1
Fort Pierce, FL 33450

Anaglypta and lincrusta wallcoverings.

Sherle Wagner, Inc.
60 East 57th Street
New York, NY 10022

Bathroom fixtures and hand-painted
basins.

Silverton Victorian Millwork
P.O. Box 2987
Durango, CO 81302

Handcrafted Victorian wood moldings,
doors, gingerbread, wainscot.

Simpson Door Company
900 Fourth Avenue
Seattle, WA 98164

Catalog.

Somerset Door and Aluminum Company
P.O. Box 328
Somerset, PA 15501

Wood millwork; windows and stairs;
  custom residential historic specialists.

Specialized Metal Works
P.O. Box 1093
Saratoga Springs, NY 12886

Restoration, replication, and custom
  design in cast and wrought iron, brass,
  and bronze.

Specialty Building Company
2629 Ridgwood Road
Jackson, MS 39216

Replicate wood moldings, curved top
  windows; antique heart pine flooring.

The Stoneyard Institute, Inc.
Alan Bird
1047 Amsterdam Avenue
New York, NY 10025

Cutting, carving, and setting up of stone.

The Structural Slate Company
222 East Main Street
P.O. Box 187
Pen Argyl, PA 18072

National supplier and quarry.

Stucco Stone Products, Inc.
P.O. Box 270
Napa, CA 94559

Cultured stone; cultured stone veneer:
  cultured brick and stucco-stone
  recomposite; stone products; interior
  and exterior.

Sunrise Specialty
2204 San Pablo Avenue
Berkeley, CA 94702

Antique-style fixtures and faucets.

Terra Designs
40 Oak Street
Dover, NJ 07801

Custom handcrafted tiles.

Thomas Tisch and Andrea Lehmann
1793 12th Street
Oakland, CA 94607

Architectural and decorative glass work;
  restoration.

Transylvania Mountain Forge
Greystone Manor
2270 Cross Street
La Canada, CA 91011

European black iron and brass hardware.

Tremont Nail Company
P.O. Box 111
Wareham, MA 02571

Manufacturer of older patterns of nail cuts.

Uni-Group North America
4362 Northlake Boulevard
Suite 1
Palm Beach Gardens, FL 33410

Precast pavers, false stone finishes.
  Technical information available.

Vermont Table Company
61 Maine Street
Proctor, VT 05765

Natural stone supplier and quarries; stone
  cleaning supplies and poultices.

Vetter Stone Company
P.O. Box 38
Kasota, MN 56050

Natural stone supplier and quarries;
  information handbook available.

Victorian Warehouse
190 Grace Street
Auburn, CA 95603

Reproduction Victorian hardware,
  fixtures, doors, window coverings.

Vintage Woodworks
513 South Adams
Frederickburg, TX 78624

Victorian millwork; gingerbread, fretwork,
  balusters and posts, gazebos.

Jack Wallis Doors
Route 1, Box 22A
Murray, KY 42071

Weathercap Inc.
P.O. Box 1776
Slidell, LA 70459

Masonry joint protection systems, stone
  flashings, lead arrowheads.

J.P. Weaver
2301 W. Victory Boulevard
Burbank, CA 91506

Composition ornamental (plaster) design,
  also known as "compo." Custom cast
  stone work.

Webb Manufacturing, Inc.
1201 Maple Avenue
Conneaut, OH 44030

Winburn Porcelain Ceramic Tile Company
1709 East 9th Street
Little Rock, AK 72203

Hexagons, squares, borders, murals, trim
  shapes.

Bob Winebarger
Furniture Maker
1507 San Pablo Avenue
Berkeley, CA 94702

Architectural wainscoting and detailing;
  cabinetry.

Worthington Group, Ltd.
P.O. Box 53101
Atlanta, GA 30355

Wood columns, mantels, and pedestals.

Zepsa Woodworking, Inc.
10701-A South Commerce Boulevard
Box 1765
Charlotte, NC 28210

Architectural millwork, curved stairs,
  balustrades, and handrails.

INDEX

DATE DUE